THE BIBLE

IN

TWO HOURS

Get an Afterlife

Patriarch Publishing Company, Inc.

ISBN: 9781736651926

Interior design by booknook.biz

PatriarchPublishingCompany.com

TABLE OF CONTENTS

Look Inside/Introduction   iv

Chapter 1: Chronological Narrative   **1**
Genesis - 2 Chronicles

Chapter 2: History, Literature, Prayer & Wisdom   **43**
Ezra - Song of Solomon

Chapter 3: Prophecies   **55**
Isaiah - Malachi

Chapter 4: Gospels, Acts   **69**
Matthew – Acts

Chapter 5: New Testament Letters   **89**
Romans – Revelation

Endnotes   112

Notes   113

LOOK INSIDE/ INTRODUCTION

Who hung himself because his advice was not followed? Who had to lie down on his left side for 390 days? Who fell asleep, fell from a third-floor window and died during a lengthy sermon? Whose thumbs and big toes were cut off? Who killed her grandchildren so she could sit as king? Who was criticized in his eulogy for going to doctors when he was sick instead of praying? Which king stood still in battle and won? The Bible – it's more exciting than you think!

CHAPTER 1

CHRONOLOGICAL NARRATIVE

GENESIS

Genesis means "beginning". In Genesis God created the heaven and earth in six days. On the seventh He rested. During this period of creation He created water, light, land, plants, the sun and moon, the stars, fish, fowl and cattle. Then He said, "Let us make man in our own image". Why does God say, "us"? It indicates there were other beings at the time, most likely angels. "Evening came, then morning" was how whole days were described, indicating a calendar day was to begin at evening.

Adam, the first man, was formed from the dust of the earth. Since no other created being was compatible for him, God created Eve, the first woman, out of Adam's rib. God said He had given them every herb bearing seed and tree for food, implying they did not consume beef, fowl or

1

fish at that time. After a serpent tempted Eve, she and Adam ate from the tree of knowledge of good and evil in the garden of Eden, which God forbade, so He banished them from the garden and put cherubim and a turning sword there to guard it.

Adam and Eve bore Cain, then Abel. Cain was a farmer and Abel a herdsman. Each made an offering to God. God was pleased with Abel's offering but not with Cain's. Why the Lord was not pleased with Cain's offering is not clear. After Eve ate from the Tree of Knowledge, God cursed the ground. It is possible that whatever then grew from the ground was not appropriate to offer to God. So Cain was jealous of Abel and killed him. Cain was the first murderer in the Bible. Lamech, a descendant of Cain, was the second murderer. Lamech killed a young man who injured him. After Cain killed Abel, Cain took a wife, though her name and lineage are not mentioned. Adam and Eve had another son, Seth. Seth took a wife, whose name and lineage are also not mentioned.

Six generations after Adam, Enoch was born. Enoch did not die. He "walked with God and was not" as God took him to heaven. Enoch's son, Methuselah, was the oldest person in Scripture. He lived until he was 969 years old. Jared, Enoch's father, who gave up the ghost when he was 962, was the second oldest. One other person in Scripture did not die. Elijah in 2 Kings 2:11 went to heaven in a whirlwind.

Noah was born nine generations after Adam. He was just and perfect, and God told him to build an ark. God wanted to destroy the earth because of the wickedness of the people. So Noah, his family and two of every animal were on the ark when God flooded the earth. Every creature on earth that was not on the ark died. God told Noah that every moving thing would be food for him. This is where mankind was first instructed that meat consumption was acceptable. God made a rainbow and told Noah it was a sign of a perpetual covenant between Him, Noah and the rest of the living creatures on earth that He would never again destroy the earth with water. It does not say God would not destroy the earth by some other means. When people see rainbows they often reflect on God because of this part of Scripture.

Noah had a vineyard. He was drunk, and his son, Ham, "discovered his nakedness". The Book of Leviticus implies this meant he had sex with his mother or with Noah. Noah cursed Ham's son, Canaan, not Ham, possibly because Canaan might have been born from a union between Ham and Ham's mother. However, this incident is not entirely clear. Rashi, a preeminent commentator on the first five books of Scripture, wrote that scholars thought Ham sodomized or castrated Noah[1]. Later in Scripture Canaan's descendants settled in the land of Canaan, the Promised Land, and God gave this land to the Israelites, who conquered the Canaanites in battle.

3

Life expectancies dwindled dramatically by the time of Abraham, who was born ten generations after Noah and was 75 when God told him to go on a lengthy journey to resettle. God was going to give him the land of Canaan, the Promised Land.

God told Abraham He would make him a great nation and that all nations of the earth would be blessed through him. Sarah, his wife, was barren so she gave Abraham her maid, Hagar, who was an Egyptian. Hagar gave birth to Ishmael, who is considered a patriarch of Islam. Sarah later conceived with Abraham and bore a son, Isaac. Christianity, Islam and Judaism all trace their lineage back to Abraham.

When Abraham left the land of his fathers he and his nephew, Lot, had so much cattle they had to settle in different lands. Lot settled in Sodom and was taken captive during war. Abraham rescued him and met Melchizedek while returning. Melchizedek blessed Abraham, and Abraham gave him a tenth of everything. This is the first instance in Scripture of the concept of tithing. In Hebrews 7:17 in the New Testament it is said that Jesus is "a priest forever According to the order of Melchizedek" (NKJV). Melchizedek had no known ancestry, as he was not mentioned in any genealogies.

Lot fled Sodom when God rained brimstone and fire upon the city. While he and his family were fleeing, his wife looked back and turned into a pillar of salt. Why did the

Lord rain down brimstone and fire? The word "sodomy" implies sexual misconduct. In Ezekiel 16:49 it says the sins of Sodom were "pride, fulness of bread, and abundance of idleness" (KJV), and that they did not help the poor and needy. In Ezekiel 16:50 it adds they were arrogant and did detestable things.

After Lot fled he lived in a cave, and his two daughters wanted children. There were not any men nearby so they got their father, Lot, drunk. The firstborn lay with him and conceived while he was unaware of what was happening. The next night they got him drunk again, and the younger lay with him and conceived. Familial relations were not prohibited until Leviticus, and this could indicate the wives of Cain and Seth were also their sisters.

Abraham asked a servant to find a wife for Isaac, and he found Rebekah at a well. She offered to draw water for him and also for his camels. People often throw coins into public fountains or wishing wells, and the myth of good fortune coming from a well is from this part of Scripture. Isaac and Rebekah had twins, Esau and Jacob. Esau sold his birthright to Jacob for a bowl of red lentil stew because Esau was hungry and faint after returning from a hunting expedition. Though twins, Esau was older and entitled to a blessing from Isaac, but Rebekah dressed Jacob in disguise to trick Isaac into blessing Jacob, as Isaac was losing his eyesight due to old age. Isaac asked Jacob if he was Esau. Jacob replied, "I am" and stole the blessing of "be lord over thy brethren and let thy mother's sons bow down to thee". After Sarah died Abraham married Keturah, and they had six children.

Jacob, later referred to as Israel, wanted to marry Laban's daughter, Rachel, and agreed to work seven years to wed her. After the seven years Laban gave Jacob his older daughter, Leah, to wed because Laban thought it was improper to give a younger daughter in marriage before an older one. So Jacob worked another seven years for Laban, and Laban gave him Rachel to wed. Jacob had twelve children, two with Rachel (she died during Benjamin's birth), six with Leah, two with Leah's maid, Zilpah, and two with Rachel's maid, Bilhah. These twelve children are known as the Twelve Tribes of Israel. Each was allotted a portion of the Promised Land, except for the tribe of Levi, who were priests. The names of the Twelve Tribes are written on the gates of the new heaven, per Revelation 21. The names of the twelve apostles of Jesus are written on the foundations of the new heaven.

Joseph, one of the twelve sons of Jacob, dreamed that his brothers would bow down to him. They were jealous and wanted to kill him, but instead sold him as a slave to the Ishmaelites, who were descendants of the child born of Abraham and Hagar. They told their father, Jacob, that Joseph was killed by wild animals. Joseph ended up in Egypt and had a place of honor in Pharaoh's kingdom because he interpreted Pharaoh's dream about wilted corn and gaunt cattle. In Chapter 2 of the Book of Daniel, Daniel also got a place of honor in a foreign kingdom after interpreting the king's dream. Joseph interpreted the dream as meaning there would be seven years of feast followed by seven years of famine. So Pharaoh, the king of Egypt, gathered grain during the seven years of feast so they would have food during the seven years of famine. During the famine Jacob, his eleven sons and their families, migrated to Egypt because they did not have food. Joseph was in charge of the food rations, and they bowed down to him in order to get food, fulfilling the dream Joseph had earlier. Joseph later made himself known to his family. He forgave his brothers for selling him into slavery, saying that God had intended to do something good all along, though selling him into slavery did not seem like a good thing at the time. This is a good story to cite when someone asks why bad things happen to good people.

Jacob blessed his twelve children before he died. Reuben, who encouraged his brothers not to kill Joseph but who had sexual relations with his father's concubine, Bilhah, Rachel's maid, was called "unstable as water". Simeon and Levi were called "instruments of cruelty". Jacob's daughter, Dinah, was raped by a man named Shechem. He begged to marry her, and the Israelites said he could marry her if all the men of the city got circumcised. But when the men were recovering from circumcision, Simeon and Levi killed all of them! Jacob blessed Judah, who was in the familial line of Jesus, by saying, "thy father's children shall bow down before thee". One of Judah's sons died before his wife, Tamar, bore children. Judah promised to give her another one of his sons in marriage but did not. She disguised herself as a prostitute, and had twins, Perez and Zerah, after Judah had sexual relations with her. Tamar and her twins are mentioned in the genealogy of Jesus in Chapter 1 of the Gospel of Matthew in the New Testament.

Jacob and Joseph died at the end of Genesis.

EXODUS

The Israelites were still in Egypt because of the famine in their land and were slaves for 400 years. They became more populous, and Pharaoh felt they could become a threat to the Egyptians. So he ordered the midwives to kill all the newborn male children of Israel. They refused because they respected God, so instead, Pharaoh ordered that all newborn Israelite males be cast into the river. God gave the midwives houses because they reverenced Him. When Moses was born his mother put him in a basket by the river. Pharaoh's daughter heard him cry, and her nurse rescued him and got his mother to care for him.

Moses killed an Egyptian who struck an Israelite, and he married Zipporah, an Ethiopian woman. When he was keeping the flock of his father-in-law, Jethro, he saw a bush on fire that was not consumed. Moses stopped, God started speaking to him and told him to remove his shoes because he was on holy ground. God wanted him to tell Pharaoh to release Israel from bondage and let them leave Egypt. Moses did not feel capable (he was the meekest person on earth, per Numbers 12:3) and asked God to send someone else. God was angry with him and sent his brother Aaron to be his spokesman.

Moses and Aaron went to Pharaoh to perform a miracle to convince him God was directing them. Aaron threw his staff to the ground, and it became a snake. But Pharaoh's magicians did the same, and he was not convinced. Moses and Aaron went to Pharaoh several times to request the release of the Israelites, and God sent over Egypt plagues of all the water in their land turning to blood, frogs, gnats, flies, dead livestock, skin boils, hailstones, locusts and darkness for three days to indicate He was commanding them. But Pharaoh's magicians were able to duplicate the plague of the water turning to blood and the plague of the frogs. And God hardened Pharaoh's heart so that Pharaoh would not allow the Israelites to depart.

God instructed the Israelites to take a Passover lamb and once slaughtered, to use hyssop to apply the lamb's blood to their doorposts. That night God passed over the Israelite homes but killed the firstborn, man and cattle, of every Egyptian family. Pharaoh then decided to allow Israel to depart. He regretted his decision and ordered his men to pursue them. At the Red Sea Moses raised his staff and the sea divided so there was a wall of water on his left and on his right. The Israelites crossed the Red Sea on dry ground, but when the Egyptians followed the sea reverted back to normal, causing all the Egyptians who pursued them to drown.

Moses was leading the Israelites to the Promised Land, and they complained. They had comfortable lives, with plenty of food and water, while they were slaves in Egypt, and many wished they would have stayed in Egypt. God sent manna and quail for them to eat. And He told Moses to strike a rock with his staff, and after he did water flowed from the rock so the Israelites could drink.

On Mount Sinai God gave Moses Ten Commandments - have no other gods before Me; do not make graven images or bow down to them; do not take the name of God in vain; keep the Sabbath holy and do all your work in six days; honor your parents; do not murder, commit adultery, bear false witness or covet. God gave Moses many other laws and guidelines regarding civil judgment and sexual ethics.

God commanded that Aaron and his sons would serve as priests, and instructions were given regarding garments, the tabernacle, worship, offerings, annual feasts and the Ark of the Covenant. The Lord gave artistic skill to Bezalel and Oholiab so they could make everything from altars to garments, indicating aesthetics were a consideration of the Lord and that it's okay to have religious images as long as they are not worshipped. Bezalel made golden images of cherubim.

LEVITICUS

Aaron was from the descendants of Levi, and Leviticus is largely a guide to priestly laws and offerings to God. There were five types of offerings - the burnt offering, the grain offering, the peace offering, the sin offering and the guilt offering. Later in Scripture it says it is better to obey than offer sacrifice (1 Samuel 15:22) and that the Lord wants "mercy, not sacrifice" (Hosea 6:6).

Permissible and impermissible foods were described. Foods including shellfish, shrimp, pork, rabbit and bats were not clean. It was also forbidden to eat fat and blood. Unlawful sexual activities were discussed further. Sexual relations with parents, aunts, uncles and animals were forbidden. If a man had relations with a virgin he had to marry her. If a woman was not a virgin and was in her father's house unmarried she was to be put to death. A rebellious, stubborn son was to be put to death. A man and woman who committed adultery were to be put to death. The annual solemn feasts were listed and included

Passover and the Day of Atonement. Modern-day readers might think some of this instruction is primitive or has ebbed in importance. But the medical community now knows that sexually transmitted diseases can kill people and cause cancer. And the Severe Acute Respiratory Syndrome (SARS) virus from 2002 and the covid-19 virus that started a pandemic in early 2020 were thought to have originated from bats, which were forbidden for consumption.

God told the Israelites not to harvest their entire land but to leave the corners for the poor. He told them they would prosper if they followed the commandments and would not prosper if they were disobedient.

NUMBERS

God told Moses to take a census, and there were 603,550 men, 20 or older in age, who could serve in the army, excluding the descendants of Levi. In 2 Samuel 24 David sinned grievously by taking a census, resulting in the death of 70,000 people.

The journey through the wilderness to the Promised Land was treacherous, and the people repeatedly complained about shortages of food and water. Aaron and his sister, Miriam, complained to Moses and asked if he was the only person to whom God spoke. God appeared to them and gave Miriam leprosy.

The Israelites were getting closer to Canaan, the Promised Land, and Moses sent twelve spies, one from each tribe, to examine the land. It was a walled city with giants as inhabitants. Ten of the men did not think they should attempt to conquer the land, but Joshua and Caleb did.

A man who was gathering wood on the Sabbath was put to death. And Moses told the people to put tassels on their clothes as a reminder to think about the Lord and His commandments. Priestly garments had tassels for the same reason.

Korah and 250 renowned men in the congregation complained to Moses that there were many just and holy people in the assembly and that more people, not just Moses, should be directing the Israelites. The next day these groups separated a short distance from each other, and God made the ground open up to swallow Korah and his followers. God instructed Moses to put twelve rods, one for each tribe, on the tabernacle. He made the rod of Aaron bud almonds. He did this in addition to having the earth swallow Korah and his followers, to show that He chose Moses and Aaron to lead the people, and no one else.

The people continued to complain, and the Lord told Moses and Aaron to speak to a rock to get water for them and their cattle. Moses struck the rock with his wand, and nothing happened. He struck it again, and water flowed. Since Moses and Aaron did not speak to the rock they were rebuked, and the Lord said neither would enter the Promised Land. In Exodus 17:6 the Lord ordered Moses to strike the rock with his wand to draw water. This time the Lord told him to speak to it, but Moses disobeyed. And in Exodus Aaron angered God. Aaron ordered the men to remove their golden earrings. He melted them and made them into a golden calf to worship. After Aaron made the golden calf, Moses, in anger, smashed the stone tablets with the ten commandments, and God had to write them on stone a second time.

The people complained more, and the Lord sent serpents that bit and killed many. Moses made a brass serpent and put it around a pole so that everyone who looked upon the brass serpent would be healed. Modern-day medical facilities often display the symbol of two serpents curled around a pole. This has its origin in Scripture.

The Lord gave instructions on how to divide the land of Canaan among the twelve tribes once it was conquered. It was well-planned with areas for foreigners and criminals.

DEUTERONOMY

Moses reminded the Israelites how the Lord had been

nurturing them on their journey to the Promised Land, the land God swore to their fathers Abraham, Isaac and Jacob. They asked Sihon, king of the Amorites if they could pass through his land along the way. He refused, they went to battle and Israel destroyed them. They then came to Bashan, and went to battle against Og, their king. Bashan was walled and fortified, but Israel conquered all sixty of its cities. In Genesis 6:4 it says the "sons of God", referring to fallen angels[2], had relations with the daughters of men and giants were born. The inhabitants of Sihon and Bashan were giants. Og's bed was more than 13 feet long. It's unclear why these giants were not destroyed by the flood in the days of Noah, though Og was the last survivor. Israel took all the cattle from Sihon and Bashan.

Moses exhorted them to follow the Lord and keep his commandments so they would prosper in the Promised Land. He reviewed the laws and commandments that were given. He told them not to intermarry with the people in Canaan so they would not start worshiping other gods. The Lord was giving this land to the Israelites not because of their goodness but because the inhabitants were wicked.

Several other laws were given. The Israelites were not to wear garments made with different materials; they could lend but not borrow; they were not to have a donkey and ox yoked together. Being unequally yoked was a term Paul used in his Second Letter to the Corinthians in the New Testament. It commonly refers to marriage between a believer and a non-believer. Just as a donkey and an ox may be likely to go in different directions, a believer and a non-believer may also.

At the end of Deuteronomy Moses blessed the twelve tribes of Israel and then died. They mourned thirty days for him. Scripture says there was never a prophet in Israel like Moses, who the Lord spoke to face to face.

JOSHUA

Joshua led Israel after the death of Moses and sent two men to Jericho to scout the land. The two stayed at the home of Rahab, a prostitute. This is the same Rahab who is mentioned in the genealogy of Jesus in Chapter 1 of the Gospel of Matthew in the New Testament. She asked the men to let her and her family live when Israel attacked, and they agreed.

The spies returned to Joshua, and Joshua led his men over the Jordan into Jericho. The priests were leading the Israelites, and when they stuck their toes in the water of the Jordan River the water stopped so they could cross on dry ground. Two other people in Scripture, Elijah and Elisha, also split the Jordan River.

Jericho was a walled, fortified city. The Lord told Joshua to command his men to march around the city once each day for six consecutive days. On the seventh they were to march around the city seven times, the priests were to blow their trumpets and then the men were to shout. After they did this, the walls of Jericho came tumbling down! The only things they were instructed to take were the gold, silver, brass and iron, which were to be put in the Lord's treasury, and the only people to survive would be Rahab and her family. It's a good question if you ask why Joshua was instructed to attack on the seventh day. Wasn't that day supposed to be a strict day of rest? There are dissenting opinions on this, and an inquisitive reader could research "lunar calendar Sabbaths".

After they conquered Jericho, Joshua said that anyone who rebuilt the city would be cursed and that his firstborn and youngest sons would die. Hiel, more than 400 years later, in 1 Kings 16:34, rebuilt the city. And his firstborn and youngest sons, Abiram and Segub, died.

The next city Joshua pursued was Ai. It was a tiny city, and his scouts told him to send just a few men. However, Ai caused Joshua's men to retreat. He asked the Lord what happened, and the Lord said Israel sinned by taking some of the plunder when they conquered Jericho. Joshua asked the people about this, tribe by tribe, and Achan admitted to taking a Babylonian garment, silver and gold, and hiding them by his tent. So all of Israel took Achan, his sons and daughters, his cattle, donkeys and sheep, and all that he had, to a nearby valley. The people stoned them and then burned them. Achan was buried under a pile of rocks. We see Scripture teach that one person's sin can affect an entire community. This occurs again in the Book of Jonah when men on a boat suffer from a tumultuous storm because Jonah disobeyed God. The Israelites were so concerned about sin that, in Numbers 15:32-36, a man was stoned to death for gathering wood on the Sabbath.

Joshua's men attacked Ai again and Ai was completely destroyed. The people of Gibeon came to Joshua and told him they were from a distant land. They said they lacked food and wanted to make an alliance with him. Joshua agreed. Shortly after, Joshua realized they were inhabitants of a nearby land. Joshua asked why they lied to him, and the Gibeonites said they feared Israel would destroy them. The people in the surrounding cities were terrified of Israel because of the miracles and power the Lord showed on their behalf. So Joshua made the people of Gibeon servants. Joshua and his men were rebuked for agreeing to an alliance with Gibeon without seeking God's counsel.

Five surrounding kings, which were kings of the Amorites, decided to attack Gibeon because they made peace with Israel. Gibeon asked Joshua to help because of the alliance they formed, and Israel defeated the Amorites in a lengthy battle. The Lord made hailstones fall upon the Amorites, and more people died from hailstones than from the sword. As it was getting late in the day, too dark for Joshua and his men to fight, Joshua told the sun to stay still. The Lord prevented the sun from going down and the moon from coming up, for a whole day, giving the Israelites time to finish the battle. There is one other instance in Scripture when God altered the movement of the sun. He made it go backwards so the shadow on the steps of Ahaz would go down 10 steps as a sign for King Hezekiah, indicating Hezekiah would live 15 more years. All in all Joshua conquered thirty one kings. Before he died he exhorted the Israelites to cleave to the Lord and not follow other gods.

JUDGES

Adonibezek was the king of Bezek, and he won seventy battles. After each victory he tracked down the opposing king and chopped off his thumbs and big toes. The Israelites defeated Adonibezek, and guess what they did to him? They chopped off his thumbs and big toes! He said, "as I have done to seventy others, so has God done unto me".

Joshua died, and the next generations forgot the Lord and were not aware of the wonders He did for Israel. They began to worship the false gods, Baal and Ashtaroth. This angered the Lord, and He aroused their enemies to attack them. When Israel called to the Lord for help, He sent judges to lead them, as they were without a leader like Moses or Joshua.

Judge Ehud delivered Israel from King Eglon by stabbing him in the stomach with a dagger. He was so fat that his fat rolled over and covered the entire dagger. Judge Deborah delivered Israel from Sisera, an army commander for Jabin, a king of Canaan. Sisera fled and Jael told him he could hide in her tent. When he was asleep she nailed him to the ground through his temples, and he died.

Judge Gideon was chosen to deliver Israel from the Midianites, whose army was too innumerable to count. The Midianites were descendants of Abraham and his wife, Keturah. Gideon wanted a sign from the Lord, so he put a piece of wool on the ground. He asked the Lord to make the wool wet but the surrounding ground dry, and in the morning it was so. The next day he asked that the wool be dry and the ground be wet, and it was so. Gideon had an army of 32,000 men, but the Lord said that was too many. Gideon said anyone who was fearful could leave. That whittled his army down to 10,000, but the Lord said that was still too many. He told Gideon to have his men drink from the nearby waters and that he would choose his army based on how they drank. Three hundred men made a cup with their hands, and the other 9,700 lapped the water with their tongues. Gideon, with just three hundred men, defeated the innumerable Midianite army. The Lord did this so they would not boast about their strength or prowess but so they would know that victory was from Him.

Gideon had seventy sons, and another, Abimelech, who was born of his concubine. Abimelech killed his brothers so he could become king. The youngest, Jotham, hid and survived. During a battle Abimelech was under a tower, and a woman dropped a stone on his head. He would have died from this, and not wanting history records to say he died at the hands of a woman, ordered his armor bearer to slay him.

Judge Jephthah was chosen to deliver Israel from the Ammonites and was the son of a prostitute. The Ammonites were descendants of Lot's younger daughter. Jephthah vowed to the Lord that he would sacrifice to Him the first thing that came out of his house if he returned from battle victorious. He had many cattle and livestock and expected one of the animals to come out first. But when he returned victorious the first thing that came from his house was his daughter. His daughter mourned for two months, and then he killed her in order to keep the promise he made to God. Scripture warns not to make vows, and this is a good lesson on why we should not.

Judge Samson battled the Philistines. He married a Philistine woman, but her father took her from him. To get revenge Samson caught three hundred foxes, tied them together by their tails, lit them on fire and released them into the corn fields of the Philistines, destroying their crop. The Philistines ruled over Israel at that time, and to avoid further conflict, the Israelites tied up Samson and delivered him to the Philistines. But he was so strong he broke the cords that bound him. Earlier he killed a lion with his bare hands.

Samson met a woman he adored, Delilah, and the Philistines enticed her to tell them the secret of his great strength. They cut his hair while he was sleeping, and he became weak. Samson revealed to Delilah this secret of his strength shortly after he went to a prostitute, indicating that sin and promiscuity can distort a person's judgment and cause God to flee, as the Lord "departed from" Samson in Judges 16:20. The Philistines then captured him and gouged out his eyes. While they were torturing Samson, he leaned against two temple pillars and prayed for one last burst of strength. The Lord allowed him to knock down the pillars, causing the roof to collapse and kill the three thousand Philistines who were watching. Samson also died in the rubble.

At the end of Judges a Levite and his concubine were visiting the land of the Benjamites. The men of the city gang-raped the concubine, and she died. The Levite chopped up her body into twelve pieces and sent them throughout Israel, one part to each tribe. The rest of Israel was furious with the Benjamites. They attacked the Benjamites, killing all except six hundred men who fled into the wilderness.

RUTH

An Israelite family, Elimelech, his wife Naomi and their two sons, moved to Moab, an enemy of Israel, because of a famine. Moabites were not allowed in the congregation of Israel (Deuteronomy 23) because the king of Moab sent Balaam to curse Israel when Israel wanted to pass through its land in Numbers. The sons of Elimelech and Naomi married Moabite women, and one was named Ruth. After Elimelech and his two sons died, Ruth escorted Naomi back to her homeland of Judah. Naomi expected Ruth to return to Moab, but she preferred to stay with and care for Naomi. Ruth married Boaz, a relative of Elimelech, and she is mentioned in the genealogy of Jesus in Chapter 1 of the Gospel of Matthew.

1 SAMUEL

Hannah was barren. She prayed for a son and said she would give him to the Lord. She and her husband Elkanah bore Samuel, and after nurturing him sent him to live in the temple when Eli was priest. Eli's sons, Hophni and Phinehas, were evil, and Eli was rebuked for not disciplining them. They had sex with women who came to the assembly and took a larger part of the offerings than what was specified in the law. Samuel had a vision and told

Eli his sons would die. In a battle against the Philistines Eli's sons were killed, and the Ark of the Covenant, which contained the tablets on which the Lord wrote the ten commandments, was taken. When Eli heard this he fell off his chair, his neck broke and he died. He was very fat from indulging on the offerings.

The Philistines brought the Ark to their god, Dagon. When it was before him his head and hands fell off. The Philistines sent it to other cities, but the people were afflicted with tumors and rats damaged their land. They sent it back to Israel. There were laws on how to reverence and carry the Ark, and 70 Israelites died from looking at it or handling it improperly. The Israelites put away their false gods, fasted and confessed. The Philistines attacked them and were defeated.

Israel sinned by asking for a king because the Lord did so many incredible things for them regardless of who was leading them. So Samuel told them they would get a king who would oppress them. He anointed Saul, the first king of Israel.

Before a battle with the Amalekites God instructed Saul to destroy everything. But he did not destroy the best of the sheep and cattle, thus disobeying the Lord. Saul also set up a monument to himself. God told Samuel to go to Bethlehem to anoint another king. He was at the house of Jesse and after seeing his first son, Eliab, thought with certainty that he was the Lord's chosen. But the Lord said

He had not selected Eliab. Jesus said not to judge others in His Sermon on the Mount in Matthew 5-7, and we see that even Samuel, a prophet, can judge people incorrectly. After seeing seven of Jesse's sons Samuel asked if there were any others. Jesse said there was one tending sheep, David, and when Samuel saw him the Lord said David would be the next king. Saul's attendants said Saul had an evil spirit, so they sought a harp player. David was brought to Saul to play the harp, and when Saul was troubled by the evil spirit David played the harp to chase it away.

The Philistine giant, Goliath, taunted Israel for 40 days. David engaged Goliath, who was over nine feet tall and had over 150 pounds of armor, in battle. David slung a stone at him, and it went into Goliath's forehead, knocking him unconscious. David took Goliath's sword and cut off his head. It was not unusual for someone with a sling to have pinpoint accuracy. In Judges, 700 men from the tribe of Benjamin, all left-handed, were able to sling a stone with the accuracy of the width of a hair (Judges 20:16).

When Saul and David returned from battle the women chanted that David had killed tens of thousands and Saul had killed thousands. So Saul was jealous of David and wanted to kill him. He tried to spear him but missed three times, and his spear got stuck in a wall. Saul told his son, Jonathan to kill David. But they were close friends, and Jonathan helped David escape. David's wife Michel, who was Saul's daughter, also helped him escape. Saul ordered his servant, Doeg, to kill eighty-five priests because Saul thought they were on David's side. David fled and was hiding in a cave when Saul entered. He cut off a piece of Saul's robe without Saul knowing it. He later showed this to Saul and said he would not kill the Lord's anointed, even though Saul was trying to kill him. Another time David came upon Saul when he and his men were sleeping. Saul's sword was in the ground by his side, and David took it rather than kill him.

The Philistines were about to attack Israel. Saul called to the Lord for direction, but because of his disobedience there was no answer. Samuel had died, so Saul went to the Witch of Endor to seek guidance. He asked her to raise Samuel from the dead, and she shrieked in horror when he arose. Samuel told Saul that he and his sons would die the next day. During the battle, Saul asked his armor bearer to kill him. He refused, so Saul fell upon his own sword. This implies Saul killed himself. But in 2 Samuel an Amalekite man told David he killed Saul after Saul wounded himself and was asked by Saul to kill him. David ordered a servant to kill the Amalekite, since the man killed the Lord's anointed.

2 SAMUEL

David asked if there was anyone left in Jonathan's family

to whom he could show kindness because Jonathan was such a good friend and helper. Jonathan's son, Mephibosheth, who was crippled in both feet, was alive, and David gave him a place at his table as if he were one of David's own sons.

David remained in Jerusalem during a battle, and from his rooftop saw an attractive woman, Bathsheba, bathing. He summoned her, had sex with her, and she later notified him she was pregnant. Her husband, Uriah, was in David's army, and David tried twice to get him to leave the battlefield and go home for a day or two. He wanted Uriah to have sexual relations with her so they would think Uriah was the father of the baby. But Uriah was loyal to the army and would not go home. So David told Joab, the leader of the army, to put Uriah in a place on the battlefield where he was likely to be killed. Uriah died in battle, David married Bathsheba, and the child died shortly after birth.

Nathan, a prophet, made David realize he did an evil thing. God forgave him but said He would raise up evil against him from his own house. This is an important lesson from Scripture. Even though someone is forgiven, the consequences of their sins can remain and be devastating.

The evil began when Amnon, a son of David, raped his sister, Tamar. Absalom, another of David's sons and Tamar's brother, killed Amnon in revenge. In an attempt to overthrow David, Absalom prepared chariots and horses and set them up by the city gate so that anyone who came to seek the king's counsel would be met by Absalom. Absalom gave advice and was acting like the king, and many started to follow him. His adviser, Ahithophel, suggested he sleep with David's concubine, which he did. Shortly after David's encounter with Bathsheba, the Lord said David committed that horrible sin in secret but that someone else would lay with his wives in broad daylight. Absalom sleeping with David's concubine fulfilled the Lord's word.

Ahithophel advised Absalom to take 12,000 men and pursue David that night because David would be weary. Absalom sought advice from another adviser, Hushai, who counselled to pursue David with all the men of Israel. Absalom gathered all the men of Israel, and Ahithophel hung himself because his advice was not followed. Scripture says Ahithophel's advice was good, but apparently it was not yet the will of God for David to die. (One other person in Scripture hung himself. Judas, in the Gospel of Matthew in the New Testament, hung himself after he identified Jesus to those who would crucify Him.)

David's men were in pursuit of Absalom and his men, and Absalom got stuck in an oak tree. His hair was so long it got entwined around a branch. (His hair weighed 200 shekels - about five pounds, 2 Samuel 14:26). Absalom's mule continued walking, but Absalom was suspended in the air, hanging from the tree by his hair. Joab, David's commander, found Absalom and thrust three spears into his heart, and he died. David mourned greatly.

Sheba amassed many followers and tried to overthrow David. Joab and his men pursued him, and he was hiding in a walled city. They started to break down the walls when a woman asked Joab why he was attacking a city that was faithful to Israel. Joab told her they only wanted Sheba, and she notified the people of the city. They cut off Sheba's head and threw it over the fortified wall to Joab.

David ordered a census and realized he sinned grievously by doing this. The prophet, Gad, told him he could choose his punishment - three years of famine, three months of his enemies chasing him or three days of plague. He chose the plague, and 70,000 Israelites died. Why was it such a grievous sin to order a census? God had done so many miraculous and great things for Israel. He split the Red Sea so they could cross it on dry ground when they fled Egypt. He made water come out of rocks twice. They conquered the kingdoms of Sihon and Og. He made the waters of the Jordan River stop so they could cross into the Promised Land. He made the walls of Jericho come tumbling down after the people marched around the city, blew their trumpets and shouted. The Lord killed more people with hailstones in Joshua's battle against the Amorites than Joshua's men killed with their swords. He kept the sun from going down for an entire day because Joshua needed more daylight time in battle. He had

Gideon's tiny army of 300, who were chosen by how they drank water, defeat the innumerable Midianite army. Despite these miraculous signs, David acted as if his success in battle and prosperity were due to himself and not the Lord.

1 KINGS

David was near death, and his son Adonijah acted as king. But David told Zadok the priest and Nathan the prophet to anoint Solomon as king. Adonijah said he would be loyal to Solomon but had Bathsheba, Solomon's mother, ask Solomon if he could wed Abishag, a wife of David. This would make him king, and Solomon seeing his deceptive intentions ordered Benaiah to kill him.

The Lord appeared to Solomon in a dream and gave him one wish. Solomon asked for wisdom so he could govern the people well and distinguish between right and wrong. It pleased the Lord that he did not ask for wealth, a long life, harm to his enemies or anything that implied greed. So He granted Solomon wisdom, riches and honor. Two prostitutes who each had newborns came to him. One slept on her child and killed it. She stole the other's baby but said it was hers. They disputed over to whom the baby belonged, so Solomon asked them to bring him a sword. He said he would chop the baby into two parts and give half to each. One woman agreed to his solution. The other said to give it to her so the baby would live. Solomon took the baby and gave it to the one who wanted it to live, concluding she was the child's true mother.

Solomon's wisdom exceeded the wisdom of all the people of the east and all the people of Egypt. Kings and peoples from all nations came to listen to the wisdom of Solomon.

David wanted to build a temple for the Lord. But he shed too much blood in the Lord's sight, so Solomon built the temple. It was an extraordinary feat, taking seven years to complete. The wood was sent from Hiram, king of Tyre, by sea. And there were 80,000 workers who were responsible for cutting stone. When the temple was dedicated, Solomon offered 22,000 cattle and 120,000 sheep and goats. After the completion of the temple Solomon built his own palace, which took thirteen years.

The Queen of Sheba came to visit Solomon. He answered all her questions, and she gave him gold, spices and stones. The amount of gold Solomon received each year was 666 talents. In Chapter 13 of the Book of Revelation the number 666 is associated with an end-of-times prophecy. It refers to a second beast and is the number of a man who makes war against the Lord and His followers. (The number 666 is also mentioned in Ezra. Adonikam had 666 children who returned to Jerusalem from the Babylonian captivity. In Nehemiah it says

31

Adonikam had 667 children who returned.)

Solomon had seven hundred wives and three hundred concubines, and they turned his heart away from the Lord and to their gods. One of Solomon's overseers of laborers, Jeroboam, was going toward Jerusalem and met a prophet, Ahijah. Ahijah removed his coat and tore it into twelve pieces. He gave ten pieces to Jeroboam, prophesying that he would lead ten tribes of Israel. After Solomon died, Rehoboam, his son, was to be king. But the people were concerned he would be harsh on them, as Solomon was in regards to the labor they were forced to do. Rehoboam consulted the elders, who told him he should be lenient. Rehoboam also consulted his younger contemporaries, who suggested he be more harsh than Solomon. Rehoboam followed the advice of the younger and said he would be harsh. So the people from ten tribes decided to follow Jeroboam and no longer had a king from the lineage of David. Going forth "Israel" refers to these ten tribes, not the twelve tribes. Judah and Benjamin remained loyal to Rehoboam. So now there are two kingdoms - Israel and Judah.

Jeroboam made two golden calves for the Israelites to worship because he feared losing the kingship if they returned to the temple in Jerusalem. His legacy of idol worship persisted in the kingdom for approximately 200 years. A "man of God" met Jeroboam at the altar in Bethel and told him the priests would be killed upon the altar.

Jeroboam reached out to seize the man, and the Lord made Jeroboam's hand wither. Jeroboam allowed to be priests anyone who wanted, without choosing them from the Levites. Jeroboam's son was sick, and rather than ask the Lord if he would recover, told his wife to go in disguise to the prophet Ahijah. Ahijah was blind, but the Lord told him Jeroboam's wife would come to him. When she arrived he asked why she was in disguise and told her their son would die.

In the remainder of 1 Kings the stories of several kings of Judah and several kings of Israel are told. Many did evil in the Lord's sight and caused the people to drift farther and farther from the Lord.

In a battle against the Syrians, the Lord made a wall fall on and kill 27,000 men who attacked Israel. Ahab was the most evil king of Israel. Elijah, a great prophet, told Ahab it would not rain except at the word of Elijah. The Lord told Elijah to live by a brook and that He would have the ravens bring him food. The brook dried up, and the Lord sent him to a widow at Zarephath. Her son died and came back to life after Elijah prayed over him.

The worship of false gods was prevalent. Elijah was sent to meet Ahab and asked him to call all of Israel and the prophets of Baal to Mount Carmel. Elijah asked for two bulls, which were cut in pieces. Whoever's bull was ignited would indicate who followed the true god. The prophets of Baal prayed all day and cut themselves until they bled, but their offering was not consumed by fire. Elijah poured several barrels of water on his offering, and the Lord ignited it. When the people saw this they believed in the God of Abraham, Isaac and Jacob. They chased the prophets of Baal and killed them.

Ahab wanted to buy Naboth's vineyard, but he would not sell it because it was an inheritance. Jezebel, Ahab's wife, who killed many prophets, forged letters in Ahab's name to get the elders and noble people of the city to join them in a gathering. Two false witnesses accused Naboth of blaspheming the Lord. So the people stoned him to death, and Ahab took his vineyard. Elijah told him that in the place where Naboth's blood was shed that dogs would lick Ahab's blood. Ahab repented, and the Lord said He would bring evil upon Israel not during Ahab's days but in the days when his sons reigned. Shortly after, Ahab was killed in battle, and the dogs licked up his blood. Jezebel would be eaten by dogs at the wall of Jezreel.

2 KINGS

Ahaziah, Ahab's son, was the next king of Israel. He fell through the ceiling in his house and was injured. He ordered his messengers to ask Baalzebub, a false god, if he would survive. Elijah told his messengers he would die because he asked Baalzebub for counsel rather than the

God of Israel. Ahaziah sent a captain with fifty men to seize Elijah. They addressed him as Man of God. Elijah asked that fire come down from heaven to consume them if he truly were a Man of God, and it was so. Ahaziah sent another captain with fifty men, and again God sent fire from heaven to consume the captain and his men. The king sent a captain with fifty men a third time. An angel accompanied Elijah to tell him it was safe to meet the messengers and Ahaziah. Elijah asked Ahaziah why he did not inquire of the God of Israel and told him he would not recover from his injury. Ahaziah died the next day.

Elisha succeeded Elijah as a prophet. They were at the Jordan River, and it split after Elijah touched it with his cloak. He and Elisha crossed the river on dry ground. Elisha asked for a double portion of Elijah's spirit, and then Elijah was taken to heaven in a whirlwind. Elisha took Elijah's cloak and touched the Jordan. It split, and he crossed it on dry ground to return home.

Elisha did so many miraculous things. The waters of the Jordan were so bad that crops could not grow. Elisha threw salt into the waters to cure them, and the land was no longer barren.

In a battle against the Moabites, the kings of Israel, Judah and Edom needed to cross a valley. But there was no water for the people or their cattle. Elisha told them to dig ditches in the valley, and the next day the Lord filled the ditches with water.

A widow who owed debts had just one small jar of olive oil. Elisha told her to get several empty jugs, much larger than the jar, and the small amount in her tiny jar filled the jugs. She repaid her debts after selling the jugs of oil. The woman's son died, and when Elisha prayed over him he came back to life. And while friends were chopping wood to build themselves a place to live, an axe head flew off its handle into the river. Elisha threw a stick into the river, and the iron axe head floated to the top so the worker could retrieve it.

Elisha told a Syrian commander, Naaman, to wash seven times in the Jordan to cure his leprosy. He complained at first but then washed seven times in the Jordan and was healed. Naaman said he now knew there was no god in all the earth except for the God of Israel. He wanted to pay Elisha, but Elisha refused. Elisha's servant, Gehazi, chased after Naaman when Naaman departed from Elisha and asked for payment. Gehazi took payment and then became leprous. And when the Syrian army was at war against Israel, Elisha blinded them and sent them away to Samaria on a different route. Earlier, when Elisha was near the Jordan several youths mocked him because he was bald. He cursed them, and two bears came along and mauled to death 42 of the youths.

Elisha anointed Jehu as king of Israel and told him the Lord wanted him to destroy all of Ahab's descendants. Jehu killed Ahab's sons, Joram and Ahaziah, who were kings after Ahab. Jehu came to a house where Jezebel, Ahab's wife, was. The people threw her out of a window, and she was trampled to death. Jehu said to bury her, but when he returned her body had already been eaten by dogs, as Elijah prophesied. Ahab had seventy other sons. Jehu wrote letters to their guardians, who knew of Jehu's reputation because he had already killed Joram and Ahaziah. The guardians killed all seventy of Ahab's sons, put their heads in baskets and delivered them to Jehu.

Elisha became ill and died. The Moabites, who were descendants of Lot's older daughter, periodically raided Israel. One time when the Israelites were burying a dead man they saw raiders from Moab approaching and threw the dead man into Elisha's tomb before they escaped. The dead man returned to life when his body came in contact with the bones of Elisha. People in some religions venerate relics, bones or articles of clothing of people they consider dignified because of their holiness. The idea that these relics may have power comes from this part of Scripture. (In Acts 19 in the New Testament, handkerchiefs that had come in contact with Paul healed the sick and caused evil spirits to depart.)

About 200 years had elapsed since the reign of Jeroboam, and the Israelites still worshipped false gods and the golden calves he made. God repeatedly called them a stiff-necked people because they would not bow their heads to Him. In the prophetic books of Scripture many prophets were sent to the Israelites to warn them they had gone astray, but they did not repent. So the Israelites were taken captive and exiled into the land of Assyria by King Shalmaneser when Hoshea was king. Though Jeroboam died about 200 years earlier, he was still accused of causing Israel to sin. Their sin was that of idolatry, the worship of other gods. David, in contrast, committed adultery and plotted to kill the woman's husband, but the Lord said David was "a man after My own heart" (Acts 13:22, NKJV). Shalmaneser sent people from the surrounding area to live in Israel's land after they were exiled, but the Lord sent lions to kill many of them. Shalmaneser said the people did not know what the god of the land required, so he sent a priest from the Israelites to teach the inhabitants.

When a king's reign began or ended, Scripture would say whether the king did good or evil in the eyes of the Lord. There were nineteen kings of Israel after Solomon until the exile, and eighteen of them did evil in the Lord's sight. King Jehu got the equivalent of an honorable mention. He did some good by killing Ahab's descendants and all the followers of Baal, but he, like the other eighteen kings of Israel, worshipped the golden calves Jeroboam made. There was also periodic civil war with the kingdom of Judah and much mayhem in the hierarchies.

Zimri, the fifth king of Israel, killed King Elah while King Elah was drunk, so he could become king. Zimri had the throne for seven days, but the Israelites would not obey him because of his deceit. So Zimri set fire to a palace and died when it burned to the ground. Shallum, the fifteenth king, assassinated King Zechariah so he could become king. Zechariah's reign lasted just six months. Menahem assassinated King Shallum so he could become king and "ripped open" the pregnant women in a town he attacked. Shallum reigned for just one month. Pekah, a captain of King Pekahiah, killed King Pekahiah so he could become king. And Hoshea assassinated King Pekah so he could become king.

Assyria later attacked and captured fourteen cities in the kingdom of Judah. Sennacherib threatened Jerusalem, and King Hezekiah prayed for guidance. The prophet Isaiah told him not to retreat. That night an angel of the Lord killed 185,000 in the Assyrian army, and the rest of the army fled. Sennacherib's sons killed him shortly after he retreated.

Hezekiah had a skin boil, and Isaiah told him the Lord said he would die. Hezekiah prayed and recovered after Isaiah told him to rub figs on it. Hezekiah asked for a sign that he would live, and the Lord made the shadow on the steps of Ahaz go back ten steps.

Hezekiah and his great grandson Josiah, were good in the sight of the Lord. Scripture said about each that there was not a king like either, before or after him. Josiah wanted to repair the temple. He sent his secretary Shaphan there, and the priest, Hilkiah, found the Book of the Law.

Josiah led the people back to the Lord. He removed the pagan priests in the temple who burned incense to the sun, moon, stars and the false god, Baal. He destroyed the altars other kings built for other gods as well as the houses of the male prostitutes that were by the temple. Hezekiah and Josiah celebrated Passover, which had not been celebrated regularly or on a large scale since the days of the Judges.

Envoys from Babylon sent gifts to Hezekiah because he was ill. He showed them all the wealth and riches of the kingdom of Judah, and Isaiah said it would all end up in Babylon. During the reign of Jehoiachin the Babylonians ravaged Jerusalem and carried away the people and all the kingdom's wealth. Scripture teaches here not to flaunt wealth. Hezekiah showed the Babylonians everything they had, and the Babylonians stole all of it.

There were twenty kings in the Kingdom of Judah from the end of the reign of Solomon until they were exiled to Babylon. Eight were good in the Lord's sight. Athaliah was the only woman "king". Her son Ahaziah was king, and when he died she killed all of his sons except Joash, as Ahaziah's sister Jehosheba hid him. She took the throne for six years. Joash became king when he was seven years old. Josiah was king when he was eight years old.

1 CHRONICLES

1 Chronicles recaps Genesis through 1 Kings. It lists the offspring of Adam through Abraham, the children of Jacob and his sons, the kings of Judah and Israel, Saul's descendants, David's descendants and his generals, and reviews David's battles and other events of his life.

2 CHRONICLES

2 Chronicles recaps Solomon's life, the building of the temple, and the events in the lives of the kings of Judah and kings of Israel. There is much overlap between 2 Chronicles and the books of Kings.

King Asa, the third King of Judah, did good in the Lord's sight and had a perfect heart. In his eulogy he was criticized for going to doctors when he was sick instead of praying to God.

7:14 is a verse often quoted in prayers for communities and countries, "If my people, which are called by name, shall humble themselves, and pray, and seek my face, and turn from their wicked ways; then will I hear from heaven, and will forgive their sin, and will heal their land" (KJV).

16:9 indicates that God is constantly searching for people to exalt. It says He wanders the earth, or looks to and fro throughout the world, trying to find people with perfect hearts so He can strengthen them.

In Chapter 20 Judah is about to be attacked by the Moabites and Ammonites. King Jehoshaphat proclaimed a fast throughout the land and sought the Lord's counsel. The Lord told him to go to battle and just stand still. The Lord turned the attackers on themselves, and all were killed.

CHAPTER 2

ḦISTORY, LITERATURE, PRAYER & WISDOM

EZRA

Ṫhe exiles from Judah who were taken to Babylon returned to Jerusalem after seventy years of captivity. The first thing they did was rebuild the temple. There were 42,360 captives who returned.

In 2 Kings 20:17, Isaiah told King Hezekiah the people of Judah would be exiled to Babylon, and this prophecy occurred about 150 years later. In the Book of Isaiah (44:28) it says Cyrus, a Persian king, would rebuild Jerusalem and the temple. It is thought that Cyrus was so astonished to read this prophecy about himself, which was likely written more than 100 years before his birth, that he decided to release the Babylonian captives. The

Babylonian kingdom ended shortly after the handwriting on the wall was written to Belshazzar in the Book of Daniel.

Ezra was a priest, and his lineage is traced back to Aaron. He prayed for the forgiveness of the people and exhorted them to no longer intermarry. Foreign spouses, those of the lands they had conquered, too often led them to worship other gods, and this spurred the Lord to send them into exile. About 110 men had married foreign wives, and they agreed to send away their wives and children. The people recounted how great a king Solomon was but said that even he went astray by worshipping the gods of his foreign wives.

NEHEMIAH

Nehemiah was Governor of Jerusalem after the captives returned from Babylon. Jerusalem was in ruins, and the captives rebuilt the city walls in fifty-two days. Ezra read the Books of Moses to the people, since the commandments and ways of the Lord had been forgotten while they were in exile. Ezra read to them from morning to mid-day, and they wept when he finished. After realizing how they had sinned, they confessed and made a pact to follow the laws of the Lord. At evening before the Sabbath they closed the city gates so no merchants could enter.

They would not buy or sell in order to keep the Sabbath holy.

ESTHER

King Ahasuerus ruled 127 provinces from India to Ethiopia. He had a banquet and displayed the vast wealth of his kingdom. He wanted the queen, Vashti, to come to the banquet to show her beauty to the people, but she refused to attend. So the king had his men search the provinces for "fair young virgins", and they found many, including Esther. Esther's parents had died, and she lived with her cousin Mordecai, who was her guardian and who was taken into exile in Babylon. Before the women were presented to the king they were treated with a twelve-month regimen of oils, balms and perfumes to make them more attractive to the king. When the king met Esther he chose her as Queen.

Two of the king's guardians wanted to kill the king. Mordecai heard of this and notified the king, who had the two men hanged. One of the servants the king respected, Haman, wanted the people to reverence and bow down to him. But Mordecai would not. Haman found out Mordecai was a Jew, and an edict was made that all Jews be killed on the thirteenth day of the twelfth month. Esther asked Mordecai to have the Jews fast, not eat or drink, for three entire days. Haman built a garrison so they could hang Mordecai on it. He was about to kill Mordecai when the king asked him what should be done for someone the king wanted to honor. Haman, thinking the king wanted to honor him, said the person should be clothed in a robe the king had worn, ride on a horse the king had ridden and wear a crown. The king agreed, and asked Haman to do this to Mordecai. The king wanted to honor Mordecai because he remembered Mordecai warned him about the two guardians who wanted to kill the king.

At a banquet the king told Esther he would grant her whatever she wanted, up to half his kingdom. She asked that her life and the lives of the Jews be spared. So Haman was hung on the garrison he built to hang Mordecai. And an edict was made that the Jews could protect themselves and destroy any peoples that attack them and try to plunder their property. (An edict could not be revoked, so the previous edict by Haman that the Jews be killed was still valid.) The new edict that allowed the Jews to defend themselves was extended an additional day, and 75,000 enemies who attacked were killed.

JOB

Job had seven sons, three daughters, seven thousand sheep, three thousand camels, five hundred oxen and five hundred donkeys. Satan told the Lord that Job honored Him because of his possessions but that he would curse the Lord otherwise. So the Lord gave Satan control over his possessions. A messenger came to Job and told him his oxen and donkeys were taken by robbers and that the servants were killed. Another messenger came and said a fire burned all his sheep and their shepherds. A third messenger came and said the Babylonians carried away his camels. And a fourth messenger arrived and told Job the winds blew down the house of his eldest son and that all his children died. Job's reaction was, "Naked I came from my mother's womb, and naked I will depart. The Lord gave and the Lord has taken away; may the name of the Lord be praised (1:21, NIV)". A second time Satan spoke to the Lord and said Job would curse Him if he were diseased. So the Lord gave Satan control over his body, and Satan inflicted Job with painful boils from head to toe.

Job's friends, Eliphaz, Bildad and Zophar, engaged Job in discussion and said his misfortunes must be the result of his sins. Job did not think he had sinned and still extolled the Lord. He said God does so many miraculous things, and we cannot understand His ways.

The Book of Job is considered a literary masterpiece. The character of Job and the plot are consistent with the parameters Aristotle describes in Poetics of a deftly constructed tragedy or epic poem. Job asked Eliphaz if there was any flavor in the white of an egg; he said his days were swifter than a weaver's shuttle; he said he had escaped by the skin of his teeth.

At the end of the book the Lord appeared and asked Job questions no one could answer, such as, do you know how the foundations of the earth are fastened? Can you bind the constellation of stars? Do you know where the morning dew is stored? Can you roam through the world and humble all who are proud? Can you set the boundaries for the ocean's waves? Do you know how to balance the clouds so they will be garments for the sky? The Lord asked these questions so Job would know that we do not understand everything He does.

The Lord scolded Job's friends for giving foolish advice and commended Job for his wisdom. After Job prayed for his friends the Lord gave Job twice as much as he previously had.

PSALMS

There are 150 psalms in the Bible. David wrote the majority of them. Despite his sins he was a prayerful man. Asaph wrote twelve psalms. The sons of Korah wrote eleven. Moses wrote one (90). Asaph was a temple musician who was mentioned when the Levites brought the Ark of the Covenant to Jerusalem in 1 Chronicles 15. Korah was the leader of those who were consumed by the earth after questioning the authority of Moses. Many of the Psalms were sung throughout history in worship and had superscripts like, "to the Temple music director". Psalms are essentially short prayers, often used for guidance, instruction, encouragement, forgiveness, praise or thanksgiving.

Some of the themes in Psalms are:

- a person will prosper in all his ways if he meditates upon God's word and avoids the company and advice of critical and evil people (Psalm 1);
- the Lord is always present, even in times of despair (Psalm 23);
- He will instruct and teach you in the way you should go (Psalm 32);
- the ways of a good person are directed by the Lord (Psalm 37);
- if there is iniquity in your heart the Lord will not listen to you (Psalm 66);
- Scripture is a guide on how to live, "Thy word is a lamp unto my feet, and a light unto my path" (KJV), from Psalm 119, which is the longest psalm.

Psalms 8, 19, 100, 103, 111-113, 117, 145-150 are psalms of praise. Psalm 51 is David's prayer for forgiveness. In Psalm 31 David said his strength failed because of his sins; Psalms 27, 62 and 86 are psalms for encouragement; Psalm 91 is a prayer for protection; Psalms 105, 106, 107, 118, 136 are psalms of thanksgiving; Psalm 139 is on the omnipotence of God.

There is a lesser known theme in Psalms that is corroborated elsewhere in Scripture. It is "the beauty of holiness", mentioned in Psalms 29 and 96. Societies generally do not equate beauty and holiness. In Psalm 39 it says that when the Lord rebukes someone for their sins their beauty flees away like a moth. In Ecclesiastes 8:1 it says a person's wisdom will make his or her face glow. And Proverbs 3:8 says that reverencing the Lord brings health to your body and strength to your bones. Holiness has physical benefits. Maybe people would benefit by adding it to their health and beauty regimen!

PROVERBS

After Solomon requested wisdom when the Lord granted him one request in 1 Kings 3:5, it is written that Solomon wrote three thousand proverbs. He is considered the main writer of the Book of Proverbs. Agur authored Chapter 30, and King Lemuel wrote Chapter 31, which includes the characteristics of the ideal wife. Neither of these other writers is mentioned elsewhere in Scripture.

The book exhorts people to seek wisdom, "it is more

profitable than silver ... and more precious than rubies" (3:14-15, NIV). People often desire riches and honor, and the book says, "By humility and the fear (reverencing) of the Lord are riches, and honour and life" (22:4, KJV).

The book is a collection of instruction and provides practical advice for just about every situation someone may face in life:

- laziness, "A little sleep, a little slumber, a little folding of the hands to rest - and poverty will come on you like a bandit" (6:10-11, NIV);

- hard work, "the hand of the diligent maketh rich" (10:4, KJV);

- guidance, "in the multitude of counselors there is safety" (11:14, KJV);

- speaking hastily, "reckless words pierce like a sword" (12:18, NIV);

- caution in choosing friends or business associates, "the companion of fools will suffer harm" (13:20, RSV);

- talking too much, "He who has knowledge spares his words" (17:27, NKJV);

- business or personal relationships and how God can change hearts and attitudes toward others, "The king's heart is in the hand of the Lord, Like the rivers of water; He turns it wherever He wishes" (21:1, NKJV);

- parenting, "Train up a child in the way he should go: and when he is old, he will not depart from it" (22:6,

KJV);

- excessive eating and drinking, "the drunkard and the glutton shall come to poverty" (23:21, KJV);

- minding one's own business, "Like somebody who takes a passing dog by the ears is one who meddles in the quarrel of others" (26:17, NRSV);

- deceiving others, "Whoever digs a pit will fall into it" (26:27, NKJV).

Seven things are detestable to God (6:16-19), a proud look, a lying tongue, hands that shed innocent blood, a heart that devises wicked schemes, feet that are quick to run to evil, a false witness who lies, and he that sows discord among others.

Proverbs says, "the Lord giveth wisdom" (2:6, KJV). (An interesting discussion on whether wisdom can be taught is in Plato's Meno. Reference is made to certain ancient Greek leaders. Socrates asked why their children lacked moral character and good personal qualities but were experts in the skills a good instructor could impart, like horsemanship or gymnastics. Since there were not any instructors of wisdom and since people who had wisdom did not learn it, Socrates concluded that wisdom could not be taught and that when it came to someone it came by divine dispensation[3].)

Several verses in Chapter 3 are often memorized and quoted. "Let not mercy and truth forsake thee: ... So shalt thou find favour and good understanding in the sight of God and man" (3:3-4, KJV). A person who is merciful and truthful will be respected. "Trust in the Lord with all thine heart; and lean not unto thine own understanding. In all thy ways acknowledge him, and he shall direct thy paths" (3:5-6, KJV).

People who decide to read the entire Bible often start with this book. It is easy to interpret, and since it is not chronological, the reader does not need to be familiar with other parts of Scripture to understand it.

ECCLESIASTES

It is thought that Solomon wrote Ecclesiastes. It contains many paradoxical verses, such as, "For in much wisdom is much grief, And he who increases knowledge increases sorrow" (1:18, NKJV); "Do not be overrighteous, neither be overwise - why destroy yourself" (7:16, NIV)? and "the race is not to the swift, nor the battle to the strong, neither yet bread to the wise, nor yet riches to men of understanding" (9:11, KJV).

Solomon tried to find joy and meaning in life by acquiring anything he desired. He said all this was vanity and that the best we can do with our lives is to eat, drink and enjoy our work. Much of the book is on the vanity of life.

SONG OF SOLOMON

In 1 Kings 4:32 it is written that Solomon wrote 1005 songs. This is the only one in Scripture, and verses from it are often read at weddings. It is a story about an intimate encounter between Solomon and a woman. Since Solomon had 700 wives and 300 concubines (1 Kings 11:3), the identity of the woman is not clear. Solomon referred to her as a bride (4:8). Some translations say the woman is "black", and others that she was "dark" and darkened by the sun. The woman said her mother's sons were angry with her and made her work outdoors in the vineyard. This would explain why she was darkened by the sun. Referring to them as her mother's sons rather than as brothers could imply they had different fathers.

CHAPTER 3

PROPHECIES

ISAIAH

In the prophetic books of Isaiah, Jeremiah and Ezekiel, the Lord was likened to a loving parent who weaned, nurtured, instructed and guided His children, Judah and Israel. Once they were of age and prospered they divorced Him to chase after other gods and honored wood and stone objects rather than Him.

Isaiah prophesied for about 50 years in the kingdom of Judah during the reigns of Uzziah, Jotham, Ahaz and Hezekiah, in the eighth century BCE. Isaiah saw God, and an angel touched his lips with burning coals to cleanse him. He was told to prophecy naked for three years as a sign to Egypt and Ethiopia that they would be led away naked by Assyria. (King Saul, in 1 Samuel 19:24, also prophesied naked, for one day, when he wanted David killed.)

This book is a collection of prophecies about Israel,

Judah, Assyria, Babylon, Egypt and surrounding kingdoms.

There are prophecies that seem to be of Jesus. Isaiah wrote that a virgin would give birth to a child who would be called Immanuel. And he described a servant who suffered, bore the sins of the people and was killed.

The book contains additional prophecies of a new heaven and a new earth, as in the Book of Revelation. There is a prophecy on the end of the earth that says the earth will stagger "like a drunkard" (24:20).

In the final chapter the Lord says the person whom He honors is one who is humble, contrite of heart and who respects His word. It says whoever sacrifices a bull will be like one who kills a man; whoever offers a lamb is like someone who breaks a dog's neck; and whoever makes a grain offering is like someone who offers pig's blood. Consuming blood was forbidden and pigs were unclean, from Leviticus. Offerings and sacrifices were among the core teachings in the laws from Moses.

JEREMIAH

Jeremiah prophesied around the start of the seventh century BCE in the kingdom of Judah, to kings Josiah, Jehoahaz, Jehoiakin, Jehoiachin and Zedekiah. During this time Judah was exiled to Babylon. Isaiah had some encouraging news for the kings during his prophecies, as he told Hezekiah not to worry about the Assyrians attacking. But the rulers despised Jeremiah because his prophecies were morose. His general message was that the kings had gone astray and were evil, and that disaster would come upon the people unless they changed their ways.

A priest, Pashhur, had him beaten, and King Zedekiah had him put in prison. The king's officers later threw him into a deep well. He had been prophesying to them about the destruction of Jerusalem, even after they asked him to pray for them.

Jeremiah also prophesied that Judah and Israel would return from captivity. And he spoke of a new covenant where God would put His law in people's minds and write it on their hearts. This covenant is also mentioned in Hebrews and thought fulfilled with Jesus' teaching that the Holy Spirit would "teach you all things".

LAMENTATIONS

Lamentations is a short book of mourning. It recollects how Israel had been such a revered nation and now is in ruins.

EZEKIEL

Ezekiel lived in Babylon during the exile of Judah and had many visions.

God told him to lie on his left side for 390 days to atone for the sins of Israel and then to lie on his right side for 40 days to atone for the sins of Judah. During this time he could eat only bread made with wheat, barley, millet, spelt, lentils and beans. Many grocery and health food stores still sell Ezekiel bread.

There are prophecies against Egypt, the city of Tyre and other surrounding kingdoms. Israel was repeatedly called a rebellious people. Tyre was a merchant city rich from trade. It was conquered because of its pride. (Pride is when someone assigns to himself and not God excessive credit for successes or skills.) The king, who is not mentioned by name, was so wealthy he believed he was a god.

The final chapters of Ezekiel contain a prophecy on the rebuilding of the temple. In a vision he says the leaves of plants will be used as medicine, teaching that plants can have healing properties.

DANIEL

Daniel was a prophet during the Babylonian exile. In the

Book of Ezekiel it says he was esteemed for his righteousness, along with Noah and Job.

King Nebuchadnezzar summoned captives from Judah to teach the Babylonians. Among those summoned were Daniel, Hananiah, Mishael and Azariah. Hananiah, Mishael and Azariah were also known as Shadrach, Meshach and Abednego. They did not want to defile themselves by consuming the king's food and wine, so the king's servant, Melzar, let them have beans and water instead. After ten days Daniel, Shadrach, Meshach and Abednego looked better fed than the king's men.

Nebuchadnezzar had a dream that troubled him, but he could not remember any of its details. His magicians and enchanters could not reveal the dream to him, so he ordered that all his wise men, including Daniel, be put to death. Daniel and his friends prayed and the dream was revealed to Daniel. Nebuchadnezzar dreamed of a man with a gold head, silver shoulders, a bronze mid-section and iron legs, with iron feet and toes mixed with clay. Nebuchadnezzar was the head of gold; the silver represented an inferior kingdom. The bronze represented a kingdom that would rule the entire earth. And the fourth kingdom that would rule would be partly strong and partly weak, as iron and clay do not bond. After this, a large stone cut from a mountain crushed the man and was a kingdom that would never be destroyed. As a reward for providing the details of the dream and interpreting it

Nebuchadnezzar appointed Daniel ruler over the entire province of Babylon.

Nebuchadnezzar made a large image of gold and ordered all people to bow down to it when his musicians started to play their instruments. Shadrach, Meshach and Abednego would not worship it, so they were bound and thrown into a flaming furnace. The furnace was so hot that the men who bound them died. Nebuchadnezzar looked into the furnace and saw the three unharmed, along with a fourth person who looked like the Son of God. Nebuchadnezzar released them and made a decree that anyone who spoke amiss against the God of Shadrach, Meshach and Abednego would be chopped into pieces.

Nebuchadnezzar had another dream. It was about a tree that reached the heavens and was cut down. Daniel told him he was the tree and that his kingdom was coming to an end. Nebuchadnezzar became like a wild animal, lived in the forest and ate grass. His hair grew like feathers, and his nails were like bird claws. After seven years he returned to normal and was again ruler over Babylon. He made one of the most beautiful prayers of praise in the entire Bible (4:35).

Nebuchadnezzar's son, Belshazzar, became king and while having a feast a human hand appeared and wrote a message on the wall, "Mene, Mene, Tekel, Upharsin" (5:25, KJV). The king was terrified and asked Daniel to interpret the writing. Daniel said it meant he had been found wanting, and that his kingdom would end and be given to the Medes and Persians. That night he was slain. Many have heard the expression, "the handwriting is on the wall". It is often associated with an omen of misfortune and has its origin in this part of Scripture. At Belshazzar's feast they desecrated the Lord by using utensils that were taken from the temple when the people of Judah were exiled.

The king of the Medes, Darius, was new ruler and at the suggestion of his administrators who wanted Daniel overthrown, decreed that anyone who prayed to another god and not the king would be thrown into a den of lions. Daniel prayed three times a day. He was caught praying and thrown into the lion's den. By morning he was released unharmed. His accusers, their wives and children were put into the den of lions, and they were devoured.

Daniel had visions and a dream of four beasts, which represented four kingdoms of the earth. The fourth kingdom was different from the others in that it had ten kings who would destroy the earth. After the fourth kingdom he saw God, the Ancient of days, and then one like the Son of man, who was given an everlasting dominion.

Daniel had another vision, and while praying, Gabriel was sent to give him wisdom and understanding and to explain his vision. Gabriel is one of two angels in the Bible mentioned by name. Michael is the other. Gabriel appeared twice in the New Testament. He announced to Mary that she would give birth to Christ, and he told Zechariah that his wife Elizabeth would give birth to John the Baptizer.

Daniel's final vision was of a man clothed in linen, who told him more about the various kingdoms and the end of times, though Daniel did not completely understand.

In one of Daniel's visions the third kingdom was "like a leopard" (7:6). In Daniel's time there was not much heterogeneity in the populations of nations. All the people looked the same. But this third nation looking like a leopard, spotted, implies there will be substantial racial integration, with people of all nations and colors.

HOSEA

Hosea was a prophet to kings Uzziah, Jotham, Ahaz and Hezekiah of Judah, before Judah was exiled to Babylon, and to kings Jeroboam II and Jehoash of Israel before Israel was exiled to Assyria.

Israel was likened to an adulteress, whose husband, the Lord, was faithful, loving and the cause of her prosperity. But Israel left Him and sought other partners. The Lord told Hosea to marry an unfaithful woman, and he married Gomer. They separated, and the Lord told Hosea to reunite with her, symbolizing the relationship the Lord had with Israel.

There are prophecies that Judah and Israel would reunite and have one ruler. The faith of Judah was compared to a morning cloud that quickly dissipates. And the Lord said He wanted mercy, not sacrifice, and knowledge of Him rather than burnt offerings (6:6). This teaches that God is not solely a disciplinarian, but that He is pleased when somebody tries to get to know Him.

JOEL

Joel prophesied that the lands of Judah and Israel would be desolate and barren, but that the Lord would restore them. He exhorted the people to repent and return to the Lord and said that all who called on the name of the Lord would be saved.

AMOS

Amos was a shepherd who also tended sycamore trees. He prophesied during the reigns of Uzziah, King of Judah, and Jeroboam II, King of Israel, around 780 BCE. He prophesied about judgment to the neighboring kingdoms of Israel, including Damascus, Gaza, Tyre, Edom and Ammon, and about the destruction and restoration of the kingdom of Israel. Judah was criticized for being led astray by other gods, and Israel was criticized for oppressing the poor. Amos' prophecy to the priest, Amaziah, that Israel would go into exile and that their king would be killed was met with so much rage that Amos was ordered to flee the area.

OBADIAH

Obadiah's prophecy was toward the Edomites, who were descendants of Esau, Jacob's twin brother. They were rebuked for not helping Israel during the exile to Assyria.

Obadiah is the shortest book in the Old Testament, though it has an often-quoted verse, "As you have done, it will be done to you" (v15, NIV). Adonibezek in Judges was a good example of this. He was the king whose thumbs and big toes were chopped off after he chopped off the thumbs and big toes of seventy other kings.

JONAH

The Lord told Jonah to go to Nineveh, but he disobeyed and boarded a ship to Tarshish. A tumultuous storm rocked the ship, and the other people on board tried to determine who was responsible for this bad fate. Jonah admitted he was fleeing from God and told the other sailors to throw him into the sea. They did, and the storm stopped.

A whale swallowed Jonah, and he was in its belly for three days. Jonah prayed for help, and the whale vomited him onto dry land. The Lord again told Jonah to go to Nineveh, and this time he did. He warned the people of Nineveh about their upcoming destruction that was due to their wickedness. The Ninevites declared a fast and the king decreed that no man or animal eat or drink. The Lord relented and did not carry out the punishment He intended because of their repentance. Jonah was angry when the Lord decided not to punish them.

The Ninevites had been so sincere in their prayer and fasting that they actually made their animals fast!

MICAH

Micah prophesied in the kingdom of Judah during the reigns of kings Jotham, Ahaz and Hezekiah. The leaders of Judah and Israel were rebuked for leading the people astray. Priests were charging people for prayers.

Micah saw the reunification of Judah and Israel. He asked what the Lord required of the people and said it was to, "act justly, to love mercy and to walk humbly with your God" (6:8, NIV).

NAHUM

Nahum prophesied against the city of Nineveh about 150 years after Jonah. Nineveh was a prosperous city that returned to its godless ways some time after they repented in response to the preaching of Jonah.

HABAKKUK

This book is best known for Habakkuk's prayer in Chapter 3. The most quoted and memorized part is from verses 17-18, "Although the fig tree shall not blossom, neither shall fruit be in the vines: the labour of the olive shall fail, and the fields shall yield no meat; the flock shall be cut off from the fold, and there shall be no herd in the stalls: Yet I will rejoice in the Lord, I will joy in the God of my salvation" (KJV). He said to rejoice in the Lord even in times of desolation.

ZEPHANIAH

Zephaniah was a prophet in Judah during the reign of King Josiah. He prophesied of judgments against Judah, Gaza, Moab, Ammon, Ethiopia, and Assyria. He also saw a revived Jerusalem.

HAGGAI

Haggai is mentioned in Ezra and prophesied to the Babylonian captives after they returned to Jerusalem. He encouraged the people to continue rebuilding the temple. Construction was halted by decree of the king because some of the city's inhabitants complained about the reputation of the exiles' ancestry.

The Lord said they had planted much but not harvested; they ate but were not filled; they drank but were not satisfied; they dressed but were not warm. Haggai was teaching the people that no matter what they did or how much they had they would not be satisfied until the Lord was part of their lives.

ZECHARIAH

Zechariah had a vision of four horses, then four horns. An angel told him the four horns were four kingdoms that scattered Judah, Israel and Jerusalem. Then he saw four craftsmen, which symbolized four kingdoms that scattered the Babylonian empire. It is thought that these were the same kingdoms Daniel saw in Chapter 7 of the Book of Daniel.

He saw Joshua a priest, and Satan by him to oppose him. Then he saw a candlestick and a gold bowl with seven lamps on it, and two olive trees, one to the left and one to the right of the bowl. This symbolized Zerubbabel would rebuild the temple. An angel told him the two olive trees were two "anointed ones" that stood by the Lord of the earth. In Revelation 1:20 candlesticks referred to churches. The two olive trees were also mentioned in Revelation 11 and called "witnesses". They would be killed. After three and a half days they would rise from the dead and go to heaven in a cloud. Zechariah saw four chariots with horses, which the angel said were four spirits. There are similarities between this vision and John's vision of horses in Revelation 6.

There is a prophecy about a shepherd towards the end of the book that seems to be about Jesus. It mentions the shepherd was sold for thirty pieces of silver, and that the thirty pieces were given to the potter. In the Gospel of Matthew Judas turned over Jesus to his accusers for thirty pieces of silver (Matthew 26:15), and the thirty pieces were used to buy the potter's field (Matthew 27:7).

MALACHI

In Malachi the people were rebuked for offering lame and diseased animals, and the priests were rebuked for leading people astray with corrupt teachings.

It is written that the tithe was to be used to store food for the poor, not for anything else (3:10). The people were urged to remember the laws of Moses.

CHAPTER 4

GOSPELS, ACTS

MATTHEW

Matthew is the first of four gospels, all which recount the teachings and life of Jesus.

Matthew begins with the genealogy of Jesus. Many familiar people are in the genealogy, including Isaac; Jacob (Israel); Phares, Zara and Tamar (Tamar was the woman in Genesis 38 who dressed up as a prostitute, got pregnant from Judah and bore twins, Phares and Zara); David; Bathsheba, the woman who committed adultery with King David; Solomon; Rahab, the prostitute who hosted the spies when Joshua sent them to scout the land of Jericho; Ruth; Asa, the king who had a perfect heart but was admonished for going to doctors instead of praying when he was ill; Jehoshaphat, the king who won in battle by just standing still and allowing the Lord to do the work; and Zerubbabel, who rebuilt the temple after the exiles returned from Babylon. The Gospel of Luke is the only other gospel that has a genealogy of Jesus. In the Gospel of Matthew Jesus' lineage is traced back to Abraham. In the Gospel of Luke His lineage is traced back to Adam through Adam and Eve's son, Seth.

Joseph and Mary were the parents of Jesus. Mary was pregnant though they had not had relations, so Joseph wanted to divorce her. But an angel told Joseph in a dream that Mary was conceived by the Holy Spirit. The Gospel of Luke is the only other gospel that recounts the birth of Jesus. In Luke's gospel Joseph did not have this dream. In Luke the angel Gabriel was sent to Mary to tell her she would conceive through the Holy Spirit. After the birth of Jesus three wise men from the east came to worship Him, as they considered Him the newborn king of the Jews. Herod, the despot emperor, was jealous and wanted to kill Jesus. He could not locate Jesus, so he ordered the murder of all male babies in Bethlehem and the surrounding area that were two years old or less.

John the Baptizer began his ministry. He baptized Jesus and said He would gather His wheat and burn the chaff in unquenchable fire. This indicates there is a heaven and a hell, and that Jesus determines who goes where. In Revelation 5 Jesus was the only one who could open the Book of Life.

After Jesus reached adulthood Satan tempted Him by asking Him to perform miracles and by offering Jesus all the kingdoms of the world if He would worship Satan.

Jesus refuted him by quoting verses from Deuteronomy, and Satan fled. Scripture says, "Resist the devil and he will flee from you" (James 4:7, KJV).

Jesus began His ministry by calling His disciples. The first were Peter, Andrew, James and John. Multitudes of people started following Jesus because of His preaching and because He healed every disease among the people.

The core of His teaching is contained in the Sermon on the Mount, in chapters 5-7. There is another version of this sermon, shorter, in Chapter 6 of the Gospel of Luke, with additional parts in Luke 11. In the sermon He discussed many things, including blessedness, prayer, fasting, worry, anger, sin, revenge, almsgiving, and judging others. The Lord's Prayer and the Golden Rule, "Do unto others as you would have them do unto you", are in this sermon.

Jesus often taught in parables, and more than ten parables are in Matthew's gospel. There is a parable of The Sower. Some of the planted seed, like people, bear good fruit, and some bear none at all; one of Wheat and Weeds, where the good (wheat) and evil (weeds) grew together and were judged at the end of time, not presently because they could morph into the other by harvest; one of Mustard Seed and Yeast; one on finding Buried Treasure; one comparing the Lord's kingdom to a fishing net that contained all kinds of fish. Some fish were kept, and some were thrown away.

There's a parable of the Unforgiving Servant, who would not forgive his debtors though he was forgiven by his creditors; Laborers in the Vineyard, who received the same wage regardless of what time of day they went into the field to work. This is an analogy that the wage of heaven is available to everyone, regardless of when they start following the Lord. It is never too late! There's a parable of Two Sons; the Wedding Feast; one of Ten Virgins - half were prepared as they had enough oil for their lamps when their master returned. They would not share their oil with the other five who asked but nonetheless were rewarded. Christ's teachings are often about giving and sharing, but here He says that sometimes you have to say "no" to people who are careless, like the five in this parable who ran out of lamp oil. There is a parable of The Talents, where diligent people prospered and were given more, while lazy, fearful people struggled; and there's a parable of the Last Judgment, where the Lord let into His kingdom those who fed the hungry and thirsty, visited the sick and the prisoners, and clothed the naked. This parable of the Last Judgment is an ecclesiastical challenge because it does not mention prayer, fasting, tithing or religious affiliation.

Herod heard of Jesus and thought He was John the Baptizer risen from the dead. John had been in prison because he told Herod it was not proper for Herod to have his brother's wife, Herodius. The daughter of Herodius pleased Herod in a dance, and he told her he would give her anything she wanted, up to half his kingdom. Her mother told her to ask for the head of John the Baptizer, so Herod had him beheaded.

Jesus was in conflict with the religious leaders. They accused Him and his disciples of heterodox teachings and neglecting the laws given Moses. Jesus and the disciples were pious Jews; they celebrated Passover; in Luke's gospel Jesus was circumcised and presented in the temple in accordance with the laws in Leviticus. Jesus accused them not for being ritually meticulous in their worship but for having unclean hearts and neglecting the more important parts of the law, love and mercy. They sought honor and reputation, and Jesus referred to them as blind guides and whitewashed tombs that were clean only in outward appearance. Even though Jesus performed many miracles - the lame walked, the dead rose, the blind saw - they accused him of making Himself equal with God and wanted to kill Him.

The Passion, death and resurrection of Jesus followed. Accounts of these are in each of the four gospels, so to make the events easier to follow, details from each will be parsed and merged toward the end of the part on the Gospel of John.

MARK

Mark's gospel begins with the ministry of John the Baptizer. He baptized people for the forgiveness of sins and said one mightier than he, Jesus, would baptize with the Holy Spirit. Some might ask if there is scriptural basis for baptism. David wrote in Psalm 51:5, "in sin" I was born.

There is much overlap among the gospels. In Mark's version Jesus also called the disciples, healed many and taught in parables.

The Confession of Peter and the Transfiguration of Jesus are in the gospels of Matthew, Mark and Luke. Jesus asked Peter who he thought Jesus was, and Peter replied (confessed) that He was the Christ. Jesus said this was not something Peter was taught but that it was revealed to Peter by His Father in heaven. Not everything we know is taught. Only in the Gospel of Matthew did Jesus give Peter the keys to the kingdom of heaven and tell him he is the Rock upon whom Jesus will build His church.

At the Transfiguration Jesus was on a high mountain with Peter, James and John. His clothes became brilliantly white. Moses and Elijah appeared and a voice was heard, "This is My beloved Son; listen to Him" (Mark 9:7, NASB). A theophany is when a deity reveals itself to a human, and there are three audible theophanies of God the Father in the gospels. One was here at the Transfiguration; one was at the Baptism of Jesus, and the third was just before the Last Supper when Jesus prayed in John 12 that the name of the Lord may be glorified.

LUKE

The angel Gabriel told the priest Zechariah that his wife Elizabeth would give birth to John the Baptizer. He was in disbelief because of their age, so Gabriel told him he would be unable to speak until the birth of John. Gabriel appeared to Mary and told her she would give birth to Jesus. Mary visited Elizabeth while both were pregnant, and the baby in Elizabeth's womb leaped for joy. This passage is often cited by pro-life advocates. Since a fetus can express joy it is thought to be a person. Job 31:15 ("Did not the same One fashion us in the womb" NKJV), Jeremiah 1:5 ("Before I formed you in the womb I knew you" NIV), Isaiah 44:2 ("Thus says the Lord who made you, who formed you in the womb" NRSV), and Isaiah 49:5 ("he who formed me in the womb" NIV) are others supporting pro-life beliefs. There are no verses in Scripture that support infanticide, though God did not allow the son born from David and Bathsheba's first sexual encounter to live.

An angel appeared after the birth of Jesus and told the shepherds the Savior was born. Wise men from the east coming to give Him homage was unique to the Gospel of Matthew. John baptized Jesus, and the Holy Spirit in the form of a dove, descended upon Jesus.

There are additional parables, one of the Good Samaritan, in which a priest and a Levite ignored a man who was beaten and robbed, but a Good Samaritan passerby, without the priestly or rabbinical reputation for religion, stopped to help the man. There's a parable of a Rich Man who built bigger barns to store his harvest but died shortly after; one of Lost Sheep; a Lost Silver Coin; the Prodigal Son; the Pharisee and Tax Collector; The Evil Laborers; and Lazarus and the Rich Man.

The parables of the Lost Sheep and Lost Silver Coin indicate how much concern there is for just one person who goes astray or is lost.

The Prodigal Son lived in shambles after squandering his inheritance. He returned home to a great feast celebrating his repentance. This parable is not meant to trivialize sin. There are often serious consequences to sin even after someone is forgiven, as indicated from the life of King David. The Prodigal Son was welcomed back to his father's house but still lost his inheritance.

The Pharisee thought he was better than others because he fasted and paid tithes. The tax collector prayed, "Lord Jesus, have mercy on me, a sinner". He said just one sentence with the proper disposition toward the Lord and went away justified. A thief was crucified with Jesus in the

Gospel of Luke. He said, "Jesus, remember me when you come into Your kingdom". These are examples of people who prayed just one sentence with the proper disposition toward the Lord and were heard. Scripture says not to babble in prayer (Matthew 6:7), and we see it is not necessary to memorize or recite long scripts while praying.

Lazarus was a beggar. He lived outside the gate of a home occupied by a rich man who ignored Lazarus while living in luxury. Lazarus ended up in heaven and the rich man in hell. Nothing more is known about the life and habits of this rich man except that he would not share even his leftovers with Lazarus.

JOHN

In Plato's dialogue Ion, Socrates concluded that Ion, a reciter of poetry, was divinely inspired because he received prizes for speaking about things of which he had no education or training[4]. He asked Ion if a man would go to a doctor or a charioteer if he wanted advice on maneuvering a horse carriage. Following this logic, if you wanted to learn religious matters would you become the pupil of a fisherman?

This gospel begins with John, a fisherman, saying things like, "In the beginning was the Word", "the Word was God", and "the Word became flesh and dwelt among us". People think Scripture is divinely inspired because untrained, uncredentialed people like John made bold proclamations that have been quoted and read for nearly two thousand years.

In the gospels of Matthew, Mark and Luke much of the focus was on the teachings and parables of Jesus. In the Gospel of John there is greater focus on the miracles He did. The only parable in John is that of The Good Shepherd.

Jesus turned water into wine at a Wedding Feast at Cana; the bride and groom at the wedding were not mentioned; Jesus healed the dying son of a royal official; He healed a man who was paralyzed for 38 years. Jesus was criticized by the Pharisees for this because He healed the paralyzed man on a Sabbath day; and the man He healed was criticized for carrying the mat he sat on for 38 years, since he carried it on a Sabbath day. Jesus multiplied five loaves of barley bread and two fish to feed five thousand; He walked on water to join His disciples, who were in a boat on turbulent waters. He healed a blind man, also on a Sabbath day. The Pharisees asked the man twice how he was healed because they were in disbelief at the miracles Jesus was doing. They met the man's parents to confirm he was really blind from birth and were mad at the man who was healed. Finally, Jesus raised Lazarus, who had been dead for four days. Lazarus walked out of his tomb with cloth wrapped around his body.

Jesus gave discourses on the bread of life and on life-giving water. He met a Samaritan woman at a well and told her that everyone who drank from the well would thirst, but whoever drank the water He gave would never again thirst. He was so convincing she left her water pot at the well. Jesus told her all she ever did. She left and told the townspeople about Him.

Jesus told His disciples that He was the Bread of Life, and that all who came to Him would never hunger. These discourses are meant to encourage people to nourish their souls rather than their bodies. Jesus said in the Sermon on the Mount to build treasures in heaven, as they cannot be stolen or destroyed. And Solomon, who could acquire anything he wanted, said in Ecclesiastes 2:10-11 that life's pleasures were vanity. In Proverbs 23:5 it is written that wealth has wings.

Jesus did many miracles and healed numerous sick people. Still the Pharisees accused Him of violating the laws from Moses in Leviticus. Jesus said to let a woman caught in adultery go free and told her to sin no more, though the law said an adulteress should be stoned to death. Some of His healings were done on the Sabbath, which they thought violated their laws. Jesus said He and the Father were one and that He existed before Abraham. There was division among the Jews and Pharisees over Jesus. Some accused Him of blasphemy, because they thought He made Himself equal to God. Many Jews started to follow Jesus, and their priest, Caiaphas, prophesied that it would be better for one person to die rather than have the whole nation perish. So they looked for an opportunity to kill Jesus.

After the Last Supper Jesus washed the feet of His disciples and continued to preach, saying He was the Way, Truth and the Life; that no one came to the Father but through Him; that anything asked in His name would be done; that He was the vine, and as a branch cannot bear fruit apart from a vine, no one can bear fruit unless they abide in Him. He gave the commandment to love one another and taught that the commandments were given so our joy would be complete.

Judas Iscariot, the disciple who became a traitor, led the soldiers to Jesus while He was praying so they could apprehend and eventually kill Him. When He told them He was Jesus they lost their balance and fell down. In the gospels of Matthew and Mark Judas kissed Jesus to identify Him to the soldiers. Judas hung himself only in the Gospel of Matthew, after Jesus was arrested.

Jesus was scourged, whipped and hung on a cross of wood that had the inscription, "The King Of The Jews". Two thieves were crucified with Him. Both scorned him in the gospels of Matthew and Mark and did not say anything in John. In Luke's gospel one thief said, "Remember me when You come into Your kingdom". Jesus told him he would be in paradise that day. Jesus' last words in Luke were, "Father, into Your hands I commit My spirit" (Luke 23:46, NKJV). In John they were, "It is finished" (John 19:30, KJV). In Matthew many in their tombs came back to life. Joseph of Arimathea asked for the crucified body of Jesus. It was put in a tomb, and a large stone was rolled in front of the entrance.

The events of the Passion in the four gospels are similar. But in Matthew the wife of the governor, Pilate, had a nightmare about Jesus. The thirty pieces of silver Judas was paid for turning over Jesus was used to buy the potter's field, which was used as a burial site for foreigners. In Mark only, a young man followed Jesus after Jesus was arrested. The accusers grabbed the boy by his coat, and he fled naked. In each gospel Jesus' disciples tried to help Him when He was being arrested. They attacked a servant of the high priest and cut off his ear. In Luke, Jesus healed the ear; in John, Peter cut off the ear, and the servant was identified as Malchus. In John, there was not a Eucharistic Prayer/Celebration, where Jesus offered His body and blood and said, "Take, eat, this is My body", as He had given a discourse on the Bread of Life earlier in John 6. Mary, the mother of Jesus, was only present at the crucifixion in John's gospel, and Joseph, her husband, was not present in any of the gospels. It is thought that Joseph was an elderly man when he and Mary married and that he was deceased by the time of Jesus' crucifixion. According to the Protoevangelium of James, Joseph had children from a previous marriage[5]. This would explain the virginity of Mary and why Scripture says Jesus had brothers.

Three days after the death of Jesus, Mary Magdalene went to His tomb. She was alone in John's gospel and with another Mary in the other three. The tomb was empty. Two angels appeared in the gospels of Luke and John, and one in Matthew and Mark. In each gospel the stone blocking the entrance had been moved. In Matthew it was attributed to an earthquake. Jesus, risen from the dead, appeared to the two Marys, to Peter and John, to Cleopas and his friend while they were going to Emmaus, and to the eleven disciples.

In John's account the disciples were fishing and did not catch anything. The resurrected Jesus told them to throw their nets to the other side. They caught 153 fish. Jesus breathed on them and said, "Receive the Holy Spirit". Peter, the Rock of the church to whom Jesus had given the keys to the kingdom of heaven, denied knowing Jesus three times during the Passion. Peter was asked three times by Jesus if Peter loved Him. In the gospels of Mark and Luke, Jesus ascended to heaven.

ACTS

Before Jesus ascended to heaven His directive to the disciples was to instruct all nations and to baptize in the name of the Father, Son and Holy Spirit. Acts recounts the ministries of the disciples and the spread of the Christian religion.

Jesus ascended to heaven in the gospels of Mark and Luke. Acts 1:9 says He went to heaven in a cloud. The apostles were gathered together in an upper room, and suddenly a brisk wind and tongues of fire descended on them. The inhabitants of Jerusalem, which included men from every nation, came to listen to them and heard them in their native language. In Chapter 11 of Genesis the Lord confused the languages at the Tower of Babel, possibly because the laws He was about to give through Moses were meant for Jews only. Since everyone understood the apostles it seems to indicate the message of Jesus was meant for the entire world.

Peter began his ministry in Jerusalem. He addressed the men of Israel and cited Old Testament verses from the prophet Joel and King David that indicated Jesus, whom they had just crucified, was the Savior. They asked Peter what they should do. Peter told them to repent and be baptized and that they would receive the Holy Spirit. About three thousand believed Peter and were baptized that day.

After healing a crippled man and preaching about Jesus and a resurrection of the body, Peter and John were jailed by the religious leaders. They were released and ordered not to teach again in the name of Jesus.

The disciples owned everything in common and sold their possessions to give to those in need. Ananias and Sapphira withheld some of the proceeds from a land sale. When Peter confronted them over this they both fell down and died.

The apostles were healing so many that people brought the sick and those tormented by evil spirits into the streets and hoped that Peter's shadow would touch them. Thousands more believed because of the miraculous healings. The high priest and other religious leaders again jailed several disciples. But an angel opened the doors so they could escape. Gamaliel, a teacher of the Jewish law, suggested the people not obstruct the disciples. He thought their purpose would fail if it were of human origin and succeed if it were of God. The teachings of Jesus conflicted with those of the Sadducees. They did not believe in a resurrection of the dead nor did they embrace Jesus' concept that love and a pure heart took precedent over ritual. When David repented of his sins in Psalm 51 he said the Lord did not delight in burnt offerings, but that He was pleased with a humble, contrite heart.

The number of believers in Jesus was burgeoning, so the twelve apostles appointed seven deacons to assist the ministry. Among those appointed was Stephen. He did many miracles but was accused by synagogue members of speaking blasphemy against the temple and the laws from Moses. Stephen told them their fathers persecuted the prophets and that they betrayed and killed Jesus, the Just One. They cast Stephen out of the city and stoned him until he died. Stephen was the first martyr of the Christian faith.

Saul, who was present at the death of Stephen, went house to house to arrest followers of Jesus. The Lord blinded Saul for three days, and Saul then heard a voice from heaven asking, "why are you persecuting Me?" The Lord sent Ananias to him to restore his sight. Saul, later called Paul, became a convert, was baptized and began to preach in Damascus. Some Jews planned to kill him, but he escaped and went to Jerusalem.

The apostles continued to perform many miracles. Philip exorcised unclean spirits and healed several who were paralyzed or lame. Peter healed a paralyzed man and brought back to life Tabitha, a young girl.

Cornelius, a Roman officer, had a vision telling him to summon Peter. Peter, while praying on a roof, saw heaven open and heard from the Lord that it was acceptable to associate with a Gentile, or non-Jew. Association with Gentiles was restricted in Deuteronomy because Gentile religions could lead Jews away from God. Peter and some other disciples were at the house of Cornelius, and while Peter was telling Cornelius and his family about Jesus, the Holy Spirit descended upon them. Peter and the other disciples were aghast that the Holy Spirit came upon non-Jews. Cornelius, his friends and relatives were the first

Gentiles to be baptized. (An Ethiopian eunuch was baptized earlier in Acts, but it is thought he was a Jew because he was reading from the Book of Isaiah and had gone to Jerusalem to worship.)

King Herod had James, the brother of John executed, and since this pleased the Jews, the king had Peter arrested. Peter was bound in chains. But an angel freed him, and Herod ordered the execution of the prison guards. Herod, after addressing a crowd, was struck down by the Lord and eaten by worms before he died. This is the same Herod that had John the Baptizer beheaded.

The Holy Spirit sent Paul and Barnabas to evangelize in Cypress. Paul blinded a sorcerer who hindered them. A governor believed in the Lord after seeing Paul make the man blind. They went to Iconium and continued preaching in synagogues. Paul told a man crippled from birth to get up and walk, and he did. The people thought Paul and Barnabas were gods. They called Barnabas "Zeus" and Paul "Hermes" after the gods in ancient mythology. The priest of Zeus brought bulls to them as a sacrifice because he was convinced they were gods. But certain Jews captured Paul, stoned him and dragged him out of the city, thinking he was dead.

A woman who predicted the future made a great deal of money for her masters. Paul told the evil spirit to leave her, and their livelihood went away. So her masters seized Paul and his companion, Silas, and brought them before the magistrates. Paul and Silas were beaten and jailed. While in prison they prayed and sang hymns, and an earthquake caused the doors to open and the chains to loosen so they could escape. They went throughout the region preaching in Thessalonica, Athens, Corinth, Ephesus, Galatia and other surrounding cities. It is thought Paul journeyed over 2500 miles with Barnabas, Silas and other companions.

God did so many miracles through Paul that people brought to the sick and those with evil spirits handkerchiefs that came in contact with Paul. The sick were healed and the evil spirits departed.

Seven sons of a Jewish priest, Sceva, tried to exorcise demons in the name of Jesus. A demon said he knew Jesus and Paul but not them. The man possessed by that demon attacked the seven sons, and they fled their house wounded and naked. Many fortune tellers believed, as they burned their own books. So many converted that the value of the books they burned had been 50,000 pieces of silver. But the craftsmen who made false gods from silver rebelled against Paul. Their business withered as people no longer bought the idols they made.

Paul apparently was a bit long-winded in his preaching. After arriving in Greece he gave such a lengthy sermon into the night that Eutychus fell asleep. Eutychus had been sitting on a third floor window sill, and after falling asleep, he fell to the ground and died. Paul put his arms around

Eutychus, and he came back to life. Paul was beloved. As he prepared to leave Ephesus for Jerusalem the elders of the church wept.

Agabus, a prophet, took Paul's belt and wrapped it around his own hands and feet to symbolize the Jews would bind Paul in Jerusalem. Thousands of Jews believed after hearing Paul preach, but others accused him of encouraging people to ignore the laws of Moses. After Paul gave his testimony in the temple there was a dispute between members of two Jewish sects, the Sadducees and Pharisees. (The Sadducees do not believe in a resurrection or in angels but the Pharisees acknowledge both.) Still, some of the Jews seized Paul and wanted to kill him. He was arrested for causing an uproar in Jerusalem. Paul went before Felix the governor, his successor Festus and then King Agrippa, all Roman officials. They felt his actions did not warrant death or imprisonment. Paul was released, and he sailed for Rome.

The trip to Rome was over a treacherous sea. The sailors had to throw cargo overboard. They were shipwrecked three times before they landed on the island of Malta. The islanders thought Paul was a god. A poisonous snake bit him, but he was unharmed. He healed the sick father of the chief official and many others. After three months he continued to Rome and was there two years.

CHAPTER 5

NEW TESTAMENT LETTERS

There are twenty-one New Testament letters (epistles), plus the Book of Revelation. Paul authored thirteen letters. James and Jude each wrote one. Peter wrote two, and John wrote three. It's not entirely clear to scholars who wrote Hebrews. James, Peter, John and Jude were apostles of Jesus. They interacted with Him during their lives. Paul had a vision of Jesus. It's uncertain if they ever met.

These epistles were addressed to various communities or clergy typically to instruct them and encourage them to persevere amidst persecution. The evolving church faced opposition from Jews and Gnostics and needed direction regarding doctrine and worship.

ROMANS

Paul wrote this letter before he arrived in Rome. It was the final city he visited on his missionary journey in Acts, and it is thought he was martyred there.

Some of the main teachings in Romans are that the commandments are summed up in, "You shall love your neighbor as yourself". Jesus said in Mark 12:31 that this is the second commandment and that the first is, "You shall love the Lord your God with all your heart, and with all your soul, and with all your strength, and with all your mind; and your neighbor as yourself" (Luke 10:27, NRSV). (A slight variation of this first commandment is from Deuteronomy 6:5.) Paul said acting lovingly fulfills the law and does not cause anyone harm. He taught that outward observances of the laws from Moses, such as circumcision, offerings and following the dietary restrictions given in Leviticus, were only valuable if accompanied by love.

Verses 3:23, "all have sinned and come short of the glory of God" (KJV), and 8:28, "all things work together for good for those who love God" (NRSV), are among the most quoted and memorized parts of this epistle; 8:26 and 8:27 say the Holy Spirit corrects our shortcomings, and prays and intercedes for us in accordance with the will of God.

Paul urged the Romans to be spiritually minded rather than bodily or worldly minded, and to be transformed by renewing their minds so they would understand the perfect will of God.

1 CORINTHIANS

Paul spent more than eighteen months in Corinth during his missionary journey in Acts. He began ministering about Jesus to Jews, but when they oppressed and blasphemed him he decided to preach instead to Gentiles.

Corinth apparently was a rampantly promiscuous place. Paul heard among the believers of fornication, homosexuality, adultery and guys having sex with their mothers. Verse 4:4 is challenging. It says, "My conscious is clear, but that does not make me innocent" (NIV). The Corinthians thought their promiscuity was normal, acceptable behavior. Paul taught that if their moral code differed from Scripture then their moral code was errant, not Scripture. Proverbs 14:12 says this in a slightly different way, "there is a way that seems right to a man, but in the end it leads to death" (NIV).

Paul said God did not need the Corinthians to instruct Him. Job (Job 9:12) and King Nebuchadnezzar (Daniel 4:35) also said that no one can ask God if He knows what He's doing.

Paul admitted pursuing the spiritual life was difficult. He likened it to a race, which required time, effort, discipline and preparation. He exhorted the Corinthians to avoid sin at all cost because it could spread to other areas of a person's life. Paul wrote that just as a small amount of yeast leavens an entire loaf of bread, a small amount of sin

91

can corrupt a person or harm a community. And he wrote that all things may be lawful but that not all things edify.

Paul gave an encomium on love in Chapter 13. Paul listed several spiritual gifts and activities, including prophecy, faith and almsgiving, and said they were futile if exhibited without love.

2 CORINTHIANS

Paul recounted how difficult his ministry had been. He had been in prison, beaten, stoned and shipwrecked three times. He said that when he suffered he felt close to the Lord.

This epistle contains discourses on generosity and giving. Paul said the Lord loves a cheerful giver and that giving should not be compulsory.

Paul apparently had some physical deformity because he mentioned a thorn in his body (12:7). He prayed three times for the Lord to remove it. But the Lord said His grace toward Paul was sufficient.

GALATIANS

Paul visited Galatia in Acts. Galatia is where the Greeks believed Paul and Barnabas were gods because they healed the man who was crippled from birth.

The Galatian church had strayed from the faith because of heretical preachers, and Paul reviewed his own credibility to ensure them he had taught the proper gospel. He emphasized that people were not justified by observing laws from Moses but by faith in the Lord. He taught that people do not receive the Holy Spirit by works of the law.

As he told the Corinthians, he also urged the Galatians to pursue spiritual gifts rather than physical pleasures. Those following the ways of the Spirit would exhibit love, peace, joy, patience, kindness and humility (5:22). People often refer to this verse when trying to determine if something or someone is "from God" or not. It says elsewhere in Scripture (1 Corinthians 14:33) that God is not the author of confusion but of peace.

EPHESIANS

Paul spent two years in Ephesus (Acts 19:19). Ephesus is where the demon-possessed man attacked seven sons of the Jewish priest, Sceva. It is where Eutychus fell asleep, fell from a third floor window and died during one of Paul's sermons.

Idol worship was prevalent in Ephesus. The sorcerers who burned their books, which had been valued at 50,000 pieces of silver, were in Ephesus, as were the silversmiths who revolted against Paul because demand for the idols they made of the goddess, Diana, collapsed.

The church in Ephesus was one of the seven churches Christ addressed in Revelation. They did much good, but He said if they did not repent their church would be taken away.

Paul told the Ephesians of the riches of Christ and that the love of God surpassed all knowledge. He implored them to be faithful, prayerful, thankful, holy in their behavior and communication, and to be conscious of the decisions they made in their lives - as to whether they were acting wisely or foolishly.

Paul briefly discussed family life and said a husband should love his wife as Christ loved the church and gave Himself for her. And Paul advised parents to raise their children in the teaching and instruction of the Lord.

Towards the end of this epistle Paul wrote he was an ambassador in chains. It is believed he wrote this letter from prison.

PHILIPPIANS

Paul traveled to Philippi in Acts and stayed with Lydia, a merchant of purple cloth. Lydia and her family were baptized. In Philippi Paul exorcised the evil spirit from the fortune teller who earned a great amount of money for her masters. Paul and Silas were subsequently imprisoned.

Paul prayed that the Philippians would increase their knowledge so they could live fruitful, productive lives. In 2:13 Paul says, "it is God which worketh in you both to will and to do of his good pleasure" (KJV). This implies He puts His will in our hearts. Paul is teaching that God wants people to prosper and does not want anyone to wander aimlessly through life and waste their time, energy or resources. This is one of the clearest verses in Scripture on how to determine the will of God. Nonetheless listening and determining His will can be difficult. Elijah listened for the voice of the Lord while on Mt. Horeb after fleeing from Ahab and Jezebel. He did not hear it in the wind, in the fire or in the earthquake but in a gentle whisper (1 Kings 19:12).

COLOSSIANS

Acts does not specifically mention whether Paul visited the city of Colossae. It was first evangelized by the disciple, Epaphras.

In this letter Paul prays that they may be filled with the knowledge of God's will. And Paul told the Colossians that in Christ are hidden all the treasures of wisdom and knowledge.

Paul warned the Colossians not to be deceived by

persuasive teachers of false theologies. He continued with similar teachings from his other letters: to seek the will of God; to focus on heavenly rather than earthly things; to be merciful, humble, kind, thankful and earnest in prayer; to let the words of Christ dwell in them; to teach and admonish one another; and not let anyone judge them with respect to food, holy days or the Sabbath.

At the conclusion Paul wrote, "remember my chains". It is thought he wrote this letter while in prison.

1 THESSALONIANS

In Acts 17 Paul preached in a synagogue in Thessalonica that Jesus was the Christ. Many Jews believed. But the ones who did not started a riot and had Paul and several companions brought before the rulers of the city. Jason, who hosted them, paid a fine and they were released. Paul went to a neighboring city, Berea. The Jews from Thessalonica who did not believe went there to encourage the crowds to oppose him.

Paul commended the Thessalonian disciples because many had turned from idol worship. He told them they had received the joy of the Holy Spirit. The concept of joy coming from a relationship with the Lord is an overlooked and often displaced teaching. After the Last Supper in the Gospel of John Jesus told the apostles the commandments were given so their joy would be complete (John 15:11). During the reign of King Hezekiah, per 2 Chronicles 30:26, there had not been as much joy in all of Israel since the days of Solomon, which had been about 200 years earlier. What did the people do that resulted in so much joy? They celebrated Passover! Paul is teaching that if a person is not joyful, or if there is divisiveness in a family, a community or a country, it is because they have not embraced God.

There are two verses in this book that have the phrase, "the will of God". In 4:3 it says the will of God is to abstain from fornication; in 5:18 it says the will of God is to rejoice always, pray without ceasing and give thanks in everything.

2 THESSALONIANS

Paul praised the Thessalonians for their faith and perseverance through persecution and said those who troubled them would face vengeance from God.

The Thessalonians were concerned about the Second Coming of Christ, but Paul insisted it had not happened and was not imminent. The Second Coming is an idea that Christ will return after a period of extraordinary lawlessness in which many non-believers will be deceived by a leader who establishes himself as God.

Paul wrote that if anyone would not work then that person should not eat. Paul is teaching that the Lord does not want people to be lazy or selfish. In Ephesians 4:28 Paul said people should work so they will have something to give to the needy.

1 TIMOTHY

Timothy was a well-respected disciple among the believers in Derbe and Lystra, which is where he and Paul met in Acts. Timothy's mother was Jewish and his father Greek. Paul and Timothy travelled together in ministry to several cities.

Paul had high regard for Timothy. In his letters to the Philippians, Colossians and Philemon, Paul mentioned Timothy in the introduction as co-author. Elsewhere Paul said he found no one as like-minded as Timothy, who sincerely cared for the good of others.

In 1 Timothy Paul outlines characteristics of bishops and deacons, indicating structure in church hierarchy.

Some of Paul's teachings in this epistle are that the goal of the commandments is love; that people should be content if they have enough food and clothing; that they should pray everywhere and for everyone, and include prayers for rulers; it is God's will that everyone be saved; there is one mediator between God and man, the Lord Jesus; and that every creature of God is treasured.

Paul wrote that love of money was the root of all evil,

and that the rich were likely to fall into various temptations and hurtful lusts. It's not money that is evil but the love of money, since people have done unethical, illegal or immoral things to gain it.

According to the apocryphal book, Acts of Timothy, Timothy was martyred in Ephesus after trying to break-up a festival honoring a pagan god.

2 TIMOTHY

Paul wrote that the Lord gives people a spirit of power, love and a sound mind, so no one should go through life depressed, fearful or feel they cannot accomplish great things.

Paul said in the end times there would be a falling away from God, and people would become unholy, brutal, conceited, unforgiving and unthankful.

Paul told Timothy that Scripture was from the Lord and should be used to correct, reprove and instruct people in how to conduct their lives.

TITUS

Titus was a Greek disciple who traveled with Paul to Jerusalem. Titus was in Crete, and Paul directed him to appoint elders in every city there to minister to the people. Paul gave guidance on how to instruct older men, older women, young women and young men.

Paul told Titus to rebuke the many false teachers and wrote that it was better to be humble, gentle and loving than to debate religious law.

Paul consistently devalued the importance of observing the Jewish religious laws. Though Timothy was a Jew and Titus a Greek, it is somewhat of a paradox that Paul insisted Timothy become circumcised while telling Titus not to get circumcised.

PHILEMON

This is a short, one-chapter book that Paul apparently wrote while in jail, as he said he was a prisoner in Christ.

Onesimus was a servant of Philemon. He left Philemon and Paul converted Onesimus to the faith. Paul said he was sending Onesimus back to Philemon and encouraged Philemon to welcome him, though Paul preferred that Onesimus remain with him to minister.

HEBREWS

Hebrews begins saying God spoke to the forefathers

through the prophets but that now He has spoken through His son, Jesus Christ. It discusses the supremacy of Christ compared to angels, as God never said "you are My son" to an angel.

Hebrews compares the priesthood of Jesus with that of Melchizedek, who appeared to Abraham in Genesis, and that of the Levites in regards to sacrifices for sin. By sacrificing His own blood while on the cross He obtained eternal redemption for sin, whereas offerings of the blood of goats and bulls, and the ashes of heifers, did not. The foundation of a person's heart is established by God's grace, not by consuming the foods allowed in the laws from Moses.

God's covenant with Israel was that He would bless them and make them a great nation if they obeyed Him. Jews had more than 600 laws. Hebrews discusses a new covenant that pertains to all people, where God would put His laws in their minds and write them on their hearts. It's possible this refers to baptism and receiving the Holy Spirit, since Jesus said in the Gospel of John that the Holy Spirit would "teach you all things".

Jesus is said to be the mediator of this new covenant, and though His grace is abundant, it does not exempt someone from personal responsibility.

There's a discussion that attributes to faith the great accomplishments and miracles in the lives of Enoch, Noah, Abraham, Sarah, Isaac, Jacob, Joseph, Moses,

Rahab, Gideon, Barak, Samson, Jephthah, David and Samuel.

There's a jarring verse in Chapter 13, "Do not forget to entertain strangers, for by so doing some have unwittingly entertained angels" (13:2, NKJV).

JAMES

Two of the twelve apostles of Jesus were named James. The author of this letter is not the one martyred by Herod in Acts 12.

James addressed this letter to the Twelve Tribes scattered abroad, likely indicating his intended audience consisted of Jewish converts.

It is a subject of debate whether a person is justified, redeemed or saved by his faith or by his works. Paul wrote in his epistles to the Romans and Galatians that a person is justified by faith. James said faith without works was dead, and that if someone had faith it would be evident from his works. There are examples of each in Scripture. In the parable of the Last Judgment in Matthew 25, Jesus let into heaven those who fed the hungry, gave drink to the thirsty, visited prisoners and the sick, and those who welcomed strangers. This indicates works of love and charity are important. The thief crucified with Jesus in the Gospel of Luke said, "remember me when you come into

Your kingdom". This is a profession of faith without any apparent works.

James suggests using words carefully and compares the tongue to fire, which can cause much destruction. He taught that if someone does not have something he wants it is because he hasn't asked for it in prayer. He said the way to exhibit wisdom was by being humble, and that God resists the proud but gives grace to the humble.

1 PETER

Peter is the apostle to whom Jesus gave the keys to the kingdom of heaven in the Gospel of Matthew. And it was he who asserted three times during the Passion that he did not know Jesus.

Peter addressed this letter to believers in five regions of Asia-Minor. He wrote that they had an eternal inheritance in heaven and that they should rejoice in being partners in Christ's suffering, as the early church faced much persecution.

Peter, like Paul, advised people to pursue spiritual blessings rather than act lustfully, and to be holy, even in their conversations. He wrote to be humble so God would exalt them. (Moses, who was the meekest person upon the earth (Numbers 12:3), and Gideon, who said his family was poor and that he was the least in his father's house (Judges

6:15), are examples of humble people God exalted.)

Peter wrote that above all things they should love one another fervently because love covers a multitude of sins.

At the end of the Gospel of John Jesus told Peter that he would be carried away to where he did not want to go. It is thought Peter was martyred in Rome.

2 PETER

Peter wrote that people should try to participate in the divine nature by exhibiting faith, virtue, knowledge, kindness and love, and that they should obey governments; otherwise it was a sign of presumption and selfishness.

Peter said he wrote his two letters to motivate people to think before they act. He wanted his audiences to realize that either positive or negative consequences would result from the decisions they made.

1 JOHN

The author of the Gospel of John is the same John who wrote the next three letters and also the Book of Revelation. He is known as the Beloved Disciple. After the Last Supper he reclined on Jesus' chest. Just before Jesus died He asked John to care for Mary, Jesus' mother.

John tried to define the essence of God. He said God is love; and "he who abides in love abides in God, and God in him" (4:16, NKJV). The philosophy of Aristotle helps understand the essence of God. In De Anima (On The Soul), he wrote that our senses would not exist apart from external stimulus[6]. The sense of sight is stimulated by light; the sense of hearing must have sound, and the sense of smell requires odor. But love is not dependent on external influences, so it is thought to be the most godlike activity. What could God love before the universe was created? He could love Himself. Aristotle wrote that self-love is when we are generous to others, as it's honorable to do good for somebody else[7]. And God exhibited His generosity by creating mankind and allowing him to share in divine things, such as love and eternity. (The immortality of the soul is discussed by Socrates in Book X of Plato's Republic. He said things were destroyed by their own vices. Mildew destroys corn; rust destroys iron; rot destroys wood; disease destroys a body. The vice of the soul is evil. But a soul still exists after doing evil. Socrates concluded the soul is immortal because it is not destroyed by its own vice[8].)

John compared sinning to walking in darkness. On forgiveness John wrote, "If we confess our sins, he is faithful and just to forgive us our sins, and to cleanse us from all unrighteousness" (1:9, KJV). He said to avoid idols and the lusts of the world.

2 JOHN

John wrote this letter to an unnamed lady whom he referred to as "elect". The identity of the addressee is not clear.

John said he did not have a new commandment, only the one he had from the beginning, which was to love one another. He warned not to be deceived by antichrists, those who deny Jesus coming in the flesh.

3 JOHN

John addressed this letter to Gaius and encouraged him and the community of believers to do good and not evil. John condemned a church leader, Diotrephes, because he loved honor and would not accept many disciples.

JUDE

Jude's audience was a community of believers, and he exhorted them to adhere firmly to the faith. He noted that many ungodly people and false teachers had crept into the community. These people spoke abusively of religion because they were not familiar with it. In the Gospel of Matthew (22:29) it says we "err" by not knowing Scripture.

Jude made reference to a prophecy by Enoch that the ungodly would be convicted of their acts and harsh words. Enoch was the person in Genesis who did not die. This prophecy by Enoch is not recorded in Scripture. It is in the Book of Enoch, which was discovered with the Dead Sea Scrolls. The Bible references three other books that are not part of Scripture - the Book of Nathan the prophet, in 1 Chronicles 29:29, the Book of Gad the seer, also in 1 Chronicles 29:29, and the Book of Jasher, in 2 Samuel 1:18 and Joshua 10:13. (The Book of Enoch is included in the Ethiopian Orthodox Bible.)

REVELATION

Revelation is a prophecy to John that God and the righteous will triumph over Satan and evil. It's a difficult book to understand because of its symbolic literary style and because the chapters are not in chronological order. In verse 4:11 it answers the commonly asked question, "Why did God create us?" It says, "for thy pleasure" (KJV).

John saw a vision of a man on a throne surrounded by twenty-four elders, four beasts and seven angels. The one on the throne, God, had a book with seven seals around it. No one could open the seals, so it was given to a Lamb that had been slain. This represents Jesus, and only He could open the book. After He removed each seal a vision was given to John. The visions included four horses, one white, one red (signifying war), one black (famine) and one pale (death/disease). The rider of the pale horse was named Death. To them was given power to kill one quarter of the inhabitants of the earth with war, famine, disease and with the wild animals of the earth.

John saw martyrs and an earthquake that caused the sun to turn black, the moon to turn red like blood, the mountains to be removed from their places and men to be so terrified that they hid in crevices of the mountains. After this an angel sealed the foreheads of 144,000, all from the Twelve Tribes of Israel. Then John saw an innumerable number of people from all nations dressed in white. An angel told him these people survived the Great Tribulation.

After the seventh seal was opened each of the seven angels blew a trumpet. Much of the earth was destroyed. All grass burned; one-third of the trees burned; one-third of the creatures in the sea died; an angel opened the door to the bottomless pit, hell, and locusts came out to torment for five months those who were not sealed as followers of God. One third of mankind was killed, and the evil people who remained still did not repent. Two prophets prophesied for 1260 days and were killed by the beast from the bottomless pit, Satan. The evil people on earth were so happy at their deaths that they celebrated and gave gifts to each other. But after three and a half days the two prophets returned to life and ascended to heaven in a cloud.

Two signs appeared in heaven. One was a woman who gave birth to a male child, Jesus, who will rule all nations. The other was a large red dragon, Satan, having seven heads, ten horns and seven crowns on its heads. Satan was actually seen in heaven at this time but was thrown down to the earth, where he made war with those who believed in God.

John had a vision of a beast that came out of the sea. It had seven heads, ten horns and ten crowns on its horns. The beast he had just seen in heaven had seven heads and ten horns but the crowns were on the seven heads, not on the ten horns. On each head was a blasphemous name. John saw another beast, and this one came from the earth. It was like a lamb and could call down fire from heaven. Jesus is referred to as a "Lamb" throughout Scripture. In Acts 2 the apostles of Christ received tongues of "fire from heaven" at Pentecost, indicating they were given the Holy Spirit. At rites of baptism or confirmation churches call down fire from heaven in the form of the Holy Spirit, so it seems possible this beast from the earth refers to a church that is or will be apostate in some way throughout history or near the end of time. It is this beast from the earth, not the one from the sea, that forces people to receive its mark. Otherwise they cannot buy or sell. The number 666 represents the mark of this beast.

John saw a promiscuous woman sitting on a red beast. An angel told him the woman was "that great city that rules over the earth", which apparently was Rome, since the Roman Empire ruled the world at the time. Some peculiar things were said about this whore. She was "carried by" or "rode" on the beast. After the Roman Empire conquered lands its customs, including its religious customs, spread with the Empire. And the beast would "hate" this whore and make her desolate. It seems ironic that the beast, Satan or someone aligned with him, would hate what was considered a whore in the sight of God. The woman was dressed in purple and scarlet and glittered with gold, precious stones and pearls. This is nearly how the priests dressed in the days of Moses. In Exodus 28 it says the priestly garments were of blue, purple and scarlet yarn with onyx stones set in gold.

In Daniel's vision another horn arose and subdued three of the ten horns. So the world power near the end of times may be a group of ten nations that has some sort of political alliance. This horn that subdued three others is the one that wars against God and is aligned with Satan.

The evil kingdoms were destroyed. An angel bound Satan for 1000 years, then he was freed for a short time. The Book of Life was opened, and all people were judged according to their works. Among those condemned to hell were murderers and the fearful. It's intriguing the fearful receive the same lot as murderers. God made highly favorable but improbable events happen often for people in Scripture. Maybe He would have made the sun stop for them, as He did for Joshua. Maybe He would have let them win life's battles if they just stood still, as He did for Jehoshaphat. If somebody is too fearful to take just one step toward God to seek His grace, they break the first commandment given to Moses, that God is the Lord.

There's a new heaven and a new earth, where tears, death, sorrow, pain, evil and immorality no longer exist. The mysteries of God, all that we do not know about Him and His ways, will be revealed!

THE END

ENDNOTES

1 The Metsudah Chumash/Rashi, by Avrohom Davis, KTAV Publishing House, Inc.; Bereishis p.97

2 The Metsudah Chumash/Rashi, by Avrohom Davis, KTAV Publishing House, Inc.; Bereishis p.61, Bamidbar p.178

3 The Collected Dialogues of Plato, edited by Edith Hamilton and Huntington Cairns, Princeton University Press; Meno, 100b

4 Great Dialogues of Plato, translated by W. H. D. Rouse, Penguin Books Canada Limited; Ion, 540E-542B

5 Protoevangelium of James, Christian Literature Publishing Co. 1886; Chapter 9

6 The Complete Works of Aristotle, edited by Jonathan Barnes, Princeton University Press; On The Soul, Book II, parts 7, 8, 9

7 The Ethics of Aristotle, translated by J. A. K. Thomson, Penguin Group; Book IX, part viii

8 Great Dialogues of Plato, translated by W. H. D. Rouse, Penguin Books; The Republic, Book X, 607C-611A

NOTES